Scrap Your Stuff

Keepsake Scrapbooking to Capture Special Memories

 PUBLISHING

Edited by Jan Mollet Evans

MAY 25 2008

Text and Artwork © 2005 C&T Publishing, Inc.

Publisher: Amy Marson

Editorial Director: Gailen Runge

Acquisitions Editor: Jan Grigsby

Editor: Jan Mollet Evans

Proofreader: Wordfirm, Inc.

Cover Designer: Kris Yenche

Design Director/Book Designer: Kris Yenche

Production Assistant: Kerry Graham

Photography: Diane Pedersen and Luke Mulks except where noted.

Published by C&T Publishing, Inc., P.O. Box 1456, Lafayette, CA 94549

Library of Congress Cataloging-in-Publication Data
Evans, Jan Mollet,
Scrap your stuff : keepsake scrapbooking to capture special memories / Jan Mollet Evans.
    p. cm.
ISBN 1-57120-352-4 (paper trade)
1. Scrapbooks. I. Title.
TR465.E93 2005
745.593--dc22
2005017590
Printed in Singapore
10 9 8 7 6 5 4 3 2 1

Contents

Introduction

It's everywhere around us. It may be unceremoniously pushed to the back of drawers, boxed on a shelf high in a closet, pressed between the pages of a book, or lurking in the bottom of an old purse. It's not trash—it's our stuff! Those little bits of everyday life that we collect, and can't bear to get rid of, capture our memories.

We object loudly if anyone tries to throw our stuff away. It's not a half-eaten dog biscuit; it's what our baby cut his first tooth on. It's not a crumpled ticket stub from a ball game; it's Section K, Row 12, Seat 27, where I sat when I caught that foul ball. Don't use those matches…that matchbook is from the restaurant where I first met my husband!

These wonderful little bits of our personal history have a proper name—memorabilia—which empowers us to keep them. No matter how insignificant they look, these pieces commemorate those special moments in our lives, remind us of an event, or bring back memories of a particular person. Unfortunately, we don't often give our memorabilia the proper attention.

While a photo may preserve a moment with a person or occasion, our memorabilia bring back the essence of the experience. Cinnamon candies remind me of my grandmother because she always gave them to us when we visited her as kids. Uncle George always smelled of his favorite Juicy Fruit gum. I was fascinated by a small work journal that was a permanent fixture in my granddad's shirt pocket, and recently found a few pages he had written. Pillowcases that Mom embroidered have long since gone to the rag bin, but I cut off some pieces of the needlework and stashed them in my sewing box. All these things can be incorporated into scrapbook pages to give them special significance.

These are memories that a photo just can't express—looking at those stitched pieces by my mother, I get a clear picture in my head of her sitting in her favorite chair and stitching intently. I don't have any photos of that, but the "picture" is there when I see the needlework.

So look in all those nooks and crannies around your house and begin to "scrap your stuff." Whatever is meaningful to you can be included. Make a place on your pages for these great conversation starters, and journal why they are important to you. You'll discover an exciting new way to perk up your pages while featuring that stuff you've kept all these years.

Short on memorabilia? Start a new collection today, or collect and scrap as you go. Rip off a section of material from that bridesmaid's dress you wore only once, and use it to embellish a page devoted to friends. Feature a Hostess Twinkie wrapper to memorialize the year your daughter wouldn't accept anything else for an afternoon snack. Photocopy a report card to use as a background for a school picture. Anything goes, as long as the "stuff" helps to tell the stories of your life.

A Day in
Our Life

Scrapping those special days of our lives is at the heart of every scrapbooker. Of course you have pictures, but don't forget the tangible evidence. Collect memorabilia at those events to bring your scrapbook to life.

Napkins or paper plates can show the theme of a party; use a punch or die-cut machine to get interesting shapes for your pages. Babies don't wear those tiny little clothes for long; preserve a piece of newborn clothing by featuring it on a page layout. Don't forget those newspaper notices of births, marriages, and accomplishments; spray them with special acid-free treatments to make them archival.

And before you file away those official documents with the "Important Papers"—birth and marriage certificates, diplomas, licenses, and even receipts for special purchases like a new car—make copies of them for scrapping; print them out in several sizes and types of print media such as colored vellum and inkjet fabrics. Children's artwork is usually too large for a scrapbook, but copies can be made smaller and shown with a current photo for a great scrapbook story.

Think outside the box for other reminders of special days in your life.

It was love at first sight. We had exchanged glances in church for a few weeks and then one night we were introduced. We went out to eat afterwards with friends and at the restaurant he asked for my phone number. I couldn't find anything but a napkin to write on and all I had to write with was an orange highlighter that I had in my purse! Our courtship wasn't very long at all. We met in May, 1987 and married just 9 months later! At the ages of 19 and 22 our lives were taking off with plans and dreams. Big Hair and Big Dreams – now that's the 80s.

What's Your Number?

by Kitty Foster

It may look like a plain paper napkin to you, but the memento in this layout is priceless to me. After church a group of us went out to eat. My future husband went too, and during our conversation he asked me for my phone number. All I had to write on was that napkin, and I fumbled in my purse and found only an orange highlighter to write with. I collected many keepsake items while we were dating, but little did I know that my husband was doing the same. After we were married, he brought out a box of the items that he had been collecting during our courtship. I couldn't believe my eyes when I saw the napkin in there! No wonder I married him.

...from the Memorabilia Box...

Paper napkin with a phone number written on it or similar dating keepsake

To the Layout...

For Both Pages:

1. Mirror photo images in computer, and set printer media to "transparency." Print all photos in black ink on transparency film.

2. Turn transparency photos over and mount on white cardstock with spray adhesive. Trim so no edges show.

Left Page:

1. Mat the large photo for the left corner on black cardstock, about ¼" larger than the photo.

2. Mat that on the green pattern paper, about ½" larger than the black cardstock. Clip straight in from the corners of the green to the black corners to give a mitered look.

3. Apply Chalk Ink around the green edges and inside the slits on the corners of the mat.

4. Mount in the corner of the black cardstock background.

5. Title with alphabet stickers to the right of the large photo, and date below.

6. Glue second photo directly underneath the title.

7. Cut 12" × 2" strip of stripe paper, and glue to the bottom of the black cardstock.

8. Adhere 12" × 1" strip of dot paper above the stripe paper.

9. Lay napkin (or other keepsake) down, gluing at top corner.

10. Add ¼" strip of black cardstock over the seam between the stripe and dot paper, holding down the napkin.

11. Print phrases such as "big hair" and "big dreams" on white cardstock using the font LB Two Punchy. Cut near words and glue over stripe paper.

Right Page:

1. Stamp the words "in" and "the" and Chalk Ink at the upper left of the Limeade cardstock background.

2. Cut and glue a 6½" × 12" sheet of stripe paper on the right side of the limeade cardstock.

3. Mat a 12" × 6" sheet of dot paper on black cardstock and mount across both Limeade cardstock and stripe paper.

4. Mat photo on black cardstock, leaving more black at top and bottom, and adhere over the dot paper.

5. Print journaling with Smooth font on Limeade cardstock, then directly apply Chalk Ink around the edges. Adhere at edge of dot paper.

6. Cut heart out of green paper; directly apply Chalk Ink around the edges, and adhere to the bottom right corner.

7. Glue alphabet stickers for first name initials to the heart; make a plus (+) sign from skinny strips of black cardstock and glue between the initials.

8. For '80s or other decade, print in reverse on the back of the green pattern paper, using the 2PeasBillboard font. Make the ink color light gray, so it won't show through the paper. Cut out the numbers, apply Chalk Ink around the edges, then glue in place.

From Your Scrap Stash...

Multipurpose Transparency Film (3M)

Scrapper's Spray adhesive (Creative Imaginations)

Cardstock: 12" × 12" White, Limeade, and Raven (Bazzill Basics)

Patterned paper: Green Vine, Stylin' Stripes, Dot Noir (Creative Imaginations)

Colorbox Fluid Chalk Ink pad: Licorice (Clearsnap)

Alphabet stickers: Real Life ABCs (Pebbles, Inc.)

Fonts: LB Two Punchy (CreatingKeepsakes.com); 39 Smooth and 2PeasBillboard (twopeasinabucket.com)

Alphabet stamps: Typewriter (Plaid Ent./All Night Media)

Scissors

Personal Paper Trimmer (Fiskars)

A Someday Wedding

by Heidi Smith

We were young and in love and couldn't bear to wait till we saved the money for a formal wedding. So, we did what many young couples do—we got married by a superior court judge in not-so-picturesque surroundings. Only disposable camera snapshots documented our wedding, and unfortunately they looked like disposable camera snapshots. The backgrounds were awful, the color was off, and they were not very flattering, to say the least. My hope in doing this layout was to bring the emotion back into the photo and surround it with things that do remind me of that wonderful day. Transferring the photograph to fabric lessens the impact of the background and concentrates more on the emotion of the subjects…my wonderful husband and me, now more in love than ever after nine years.

...from the Memorabilia Box...

Photo snapshots, marriage certificate, newspaper announcement, fabric scrap from dress, champagne cork

To the Layout...

For Both Pages:

1. Tape canvas to a smooth, hard work surface. Be sure it is larger than the photo or document to be transferred to it.

2. Scan photo into computer or use digital photo, adjust size, reverse or mirror, and convert to black for printing. Scan marriage certificate, adjust size, and reverse or mirror.

3. Print large photo and document onto Studio Paper transfer paper with an inkjet printer. Use the settings for "best quality printing" and "glossy photo paper." Immediately take the paper to your canvas. Carefully turn the transfer paper face down on the canvas, and tape the corners down to keep it from sliding. Rub all over the back of the paper several times with a wadded soft cloth to transfer the ink. Remove paper and allow fabric image to dry.

4. Print smaller photos on glossy photo paper.

5. Reinforce 2 sheets of Rosie cardstock for the page backgrounds by gluing to chipboard with adhesive spray.

From Your Scrap Stash...

Papers: Premium glossy photo paper (Epson); mulberry paper, brown (The Paper Company); Studio Paper inkjet transfer (USArtQuest)

Cardstock: Heavy canvas, natural color, SweetPea Alyssa 12″ × 12″, 2 sheets Rosie, 1 Sprout, 1 Blossom, and a tag (BasicGrey)

Chipboard: 12″ × 12″, 2 pieces

Jump rings: nickel, brass, 10mm and 7mm (Darice)

Waxy Flax coated linen thread, Bubble Gum (Scrapworks); heavy needle

Dual-tip brush marker, Chocolate Chip (Stampin' Up!)

Pin back (Westrim Crafts)

Address rub-ons, black (Chatterbox, Inc.)

Corsage pin with pearl head

Font: Corinthian

Colorbox stylus tool and white foam blending tip (Clearsnap)

Adhesives & Preservatives: Repositionable Adhesive spray; Make It Acid-Free! spray (Krylon); Photo Memory double-sided mounting tape (Pioneer Photo Albums, Inc.)

Embellishments: Pin-tucked fabric, 2″ × 12″; Pearl—centered vintage button (The Daisy Bucket); D-ring rivet twill tape; Sheer ribbon, 2″ wide; fibers (Fibers by the Yard); Keepsake pocket, baby pink; medium brushed silver frame (Pebbles Inc.); faux diamond trim; Garden Gate designs, silk flowers (Jo-Ann Stores, etc.); shirt button snaps; garter belt attachment (Prym Dritz); silver clips; alligator clips (7gypsies); Nostalgiques by Rebecca Sower, The Attic, Paper Clips, Destinations (EK Success); pewter charms (Impress); pewter brads; antique white safety pin; Charmed Plaques, mini; cardstock tags; tiny tags (Making Memories); stainless steel tag, safety pins, rectangle frame charm (Club Scrap); Oval zipper pulls, gunmetal Life/Love (All My Memories); school clips; lacing brads (Karen Foster Design); Metal photo corners (Treasury of Memories)

Paint & Ink: FolkArt Acrylic Colors, Baby Pink (Plaid Ent.); Adirondack raised felt dye ink pad, cranberry and Archival ink, sepia (Ranger Industries)

Tools: Awl or ⅟₁₆″ punch; needle and beige or pink thread; Scotch sand paper (3M) or steel wool; X-Acto knife handle with No. 11 blade (Hunt Mfg.); Xyron sticker maker (Xyron div. of Esselte)

Left Page:

1. Trim canvas around photo, leaving a ¾" to 1" border. Use Glue Lines and a few stitches of coated linen thread to attach faux diamond trim across bottom. Attach metal photo corners to canvas. Run corsage pin with ribbon and charm through canvas. Spray adhesive on canvas back and place on page.

2. Sketch in pencil where the flowering branches will be added across the top of the page. Run tape lines over the branches you have sketched.

3. Rip strips of mulberry paper and twist into shape of each branch—the wider the strip, the heavier the branch. Press onto tape on paper. Tip: Apply a water line with a paintbrush where you want to tear mulberry paper, and it will tear easily.

4. Pull silk flowers and small leaves from their plastic stems. Add to branches using Glue Dots.

5. Ink the rings photo with sepia and cranberry inks loaded on the foam stylus; dab around the edges till an aged effect is achieved. Tip: Use steel wool to age glossy photos further; rub around the edge until the image begins to come off just a bit. Add paper photo corners, then run tape around back and press in place.

6. Tie ribbon on garter attachment and glue to top of tag and on page by photo.

7. Reverse print the title on back of Sprout cardstock, and hand cut with craft knife. Run through Xyron and attach to tag and page.

Right Page:

1. Fold over edges of pin-tucked fabric and hem. Spray back with adhesive, and apply to right side of page.

2. Mark ¾" intervals down the pin-tucked fabric about 1½" wide with a pencil; pierce holes with an awl or punch and attach lacing brads. Lace with fibers (like you would a skate) and tie at top in a knot.

3. Attach D-ring twill tape across lower half of page using mounting tape.

4. Fold a 12" long strip of ribbon into a simple envelope, shaping the flap into a triangle. Use Glue Lines and a few stitches with the coated linen thread to attach faux diamond trim across the front. Stitch up the sides with regular thread. Attach a shirt snap top to the flap and a snap bottom to the front of the envelope. Attach envelope to page with Glue Dots.

5. Trim canvas around certificate leaving ¾" to 1" border; attach to page using spray adhesive. Decorate with nailheads near corners.

6. Add memorabilia such as the newspaper announcement, photos printed very small on glossy photo paper, and a scrap of material from the wedding dress, writing on tags to identify those items. Then add charms, clip, pins, and so on, using jump rings to attach them to D-rings, and clips, pins, or glue to attach them to the laced fabric. Tie on short pieces of ribbon to accent.

7. Print or write journaling on Sprout cardstock to fit in envelope. Apply color to edges with ink pads. Fold in half, place in envelope, and snap shut.

Embellishment Notes:

■ To keep the items in the pocket from sticking to glue through the sheer fabric, dust the Glue Dot/Line areas on the inside of the envelope with cornstarch or baby powder using a paintbrush.

■ A whole champagne cork is too bulky; cut and use only a slice off the top and insert a jump ring for hanging.

■ To give metal pieces a "softer" antiqued look, before adding them to the page, paint them with acrylic paint and allow to dry slightly, then use sandpaper or steel wool to remove some of the paint and give a matte finish.

■ Get a scrap of your dress fabric from the dressmaker, or clip a small piece from the inside hem area or the shoulder pads.

■ To make the newspaper announcement or other paper or fabric items archival, apply acid-free spray to both sides.

tip

TOOL BOX:

For making holes, setting eyelets, attaching nailheads, setting snaps, and crimping metal corners, the **HomePro LR (long reach) Tool** is a great addition to your scrapping toolbox. The tool sets fit into the top and bottom of the tool head, held in place by hand-tightened thumb screws, so they are easily changed. Insert the eyelet or other metal attachment, press the handle down, and the action is complete. Available from American Tag Company.

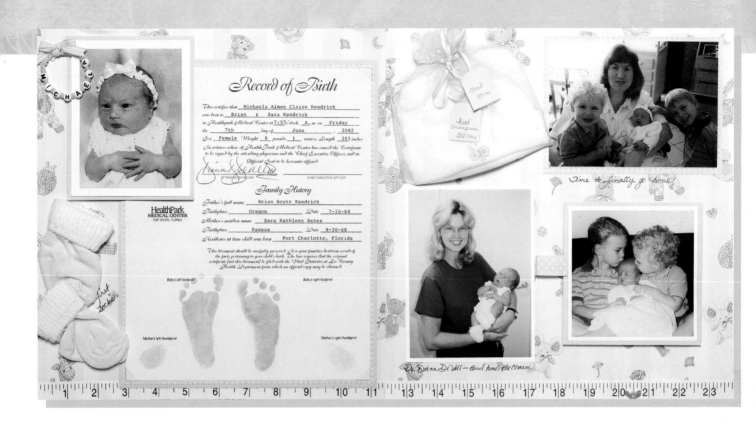

Our Baby's Birth

by Sara Kendrick

I didn't want my daughter's first precious keepsakes to be hidden in a box on some closet shelf, so I incorporated them into this scrapbook layout. Her first socks, newborn hat, hospital measuring tape, and gift and floral cards all appear here. Her record of birth and hospital photo, as well as photos of the delivering doctor and her older brothers, are showcased. Many more photos fit on this layout through the addition of my handmade mini-accordion "album."

...from the Memorabilia Box...

Baby socks, hat, and bracelet; measuring tape
from hospital; gift and florist cards

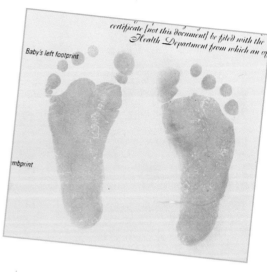

From Your Scrap Stash...

Printed papers: Cuddly Friends, Chenille Pink Dot (K & Co.)

Cardstock: Romance pink and Gardenia white (Bazzill Basics)

Jolee's organza bag, pink (EK Success)

Ribbons: pink and white gingham (Making Memories); pink with white dot grosgrain, about ½" wide (Offray)

Beads: ABCs, small pearls, small round pink (Westrim Crafts)

Wire: pink or white, fine gauge, 6" long (Artistic Wire)

Sticker: Grand Adhesions flower sticker, Cuddly Friends (K & Co.)

Pen: Lovely Lilac (Stampin' Up!)

Adhesives: Herma Dotto Permanent (EK Success); 3-D & Memory Zots (Therm O Web)

Transparent mounting corners: small (Creative Memories)

To the Layout...

For Both Pages:

1. Use permanent adhesive to attach printed background paper to cardstock for stability.

2. Adhere paper measuring tape from hospital across bottom of both pages.

3. Place Grand Adhesions flower sticker at baby's birth length on tape.

Left Page:

1. Mat birth record on dot paper with photo corners, so that it's easily removed if necessary. Mat again on pink cardstock and adhere to page.

2. Mat hospital photo on white cardstock and again on pink cardstock. Apply 3-D Zots to back of matted photo on 3 corners. Leave corner that will overlap the birth record free of adhesive. Adhere to page.

3. Using thin Zots, adhere baby socks to page.

4. Thread baby's name in alphabet beads on wire, alternating with pink beads and finishing each end with pearl beads to make a suitable sized circle. Twist together ends to secure, and cut off excess wire. Attach a pink gingham bow to cover wire ends. Adhere to layout, slightly overlapping photo.

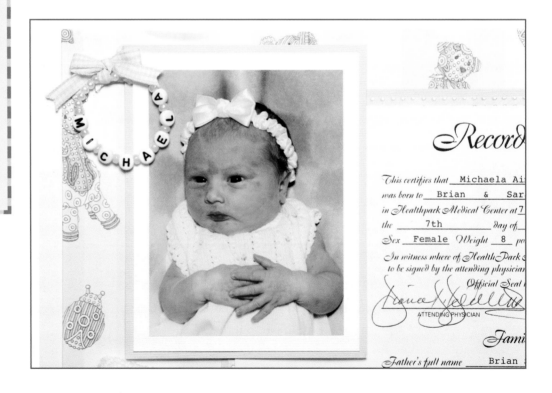

Right Page:

1. Place floral cards and baby hat in organza bag and tie loosely. Write baby's head and chest measurements on tags cut from pink cardstock; secure to front of bag with removable adhesive after tying. Adhere bag to page at upper left with thin Zots.

2. Mat other photos on white cardstock and dotted paper and adhere to layout at upper right and lower left of page.

3. Choose 5 photos and crop each to 4″ square. Mat on 4¼″ white cardstock.

4. To make mini-accordion album: Cut a piece of pink cardstock to 12″ × 4¼″. Make score lines at 4½″ and 9″. Fanfold cardstock to form book. This will leave a 3″ "tail." This tail is what you will adhere to the page.

5. Cut another piece of pink cardstock 4½″ square. This will cover the tail of your accordion book on the page.

6. Make a loop with a 3″ piece of dot ribbon by folding it in half. Adhere to the end of the accordion book so that the loop extends by 1″.

7. Use permanent adhesive to attach the tail of the accordion book to the page. Then adhere the matching pink square over the top of the tail. Mount the 5 photos that are matted on white cardstock in the accordion book, covering the ribbon loop ends.

8. Add journaling to identify photos as desired.

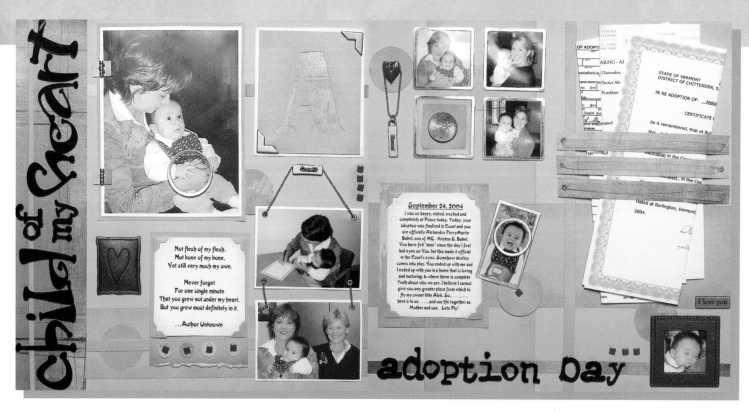

Adoption Day

By Kristen S. Babel

When I first traveled to Texas to get my newly adopted baby, Alek, I found a quarter on the ground. It was the 2004 Texas state quarter, representing the state and year in which he was born. I carried it as a lucky charm until the adoption was finalized in court. That quarter and copies of the actual legal papers I received that wonderful day are featured in this layout. Those papers made it official: I was Alekandro's mother and legal guardian. My journaling depicts the deep feelings of joy and peace that I felt, knowing that this child was mine and that we were going to enjoy our life together as mother and son.

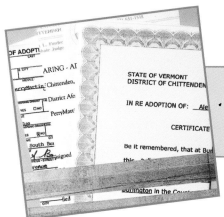

...from the Memorabilia Box...

Copies of adoption papers from court proceedings

To the Layout...

For Both Pages:

1. Use 2 sheets of Limeade cardstock for backgrounds, giving them an aged or distressed look by dabbing ink near the sides.

2. Print poem and journaling on canvas, and run ink on the edges. Add photo corners. Mat onto coordinating paper or cardstock, leaving extra space below poem; attach ½" punched paper circles below poem with brads.

3. Punch out 1½" circles and cut various widths of paper strips in colors that coordinate with your photo colors and the backgrounds; ink all edges for an aged look.

4. Arrange the paper strips with the photos to have a collage-like feel. I arrange several times before it feels right and looks balanced. Glue papers down with Glue Dots.

Left Page:

1. Mat large photo on white and Flamingo cardstocks, and run ink on the edges; set aside.

2. For the 2 photos to be "hung" on the chain: Punch ⅛" holes near each corner and attach eyelets. Insert chain through eyelets and Glue Dot in place on back of pictures. Leave enough chain at top to give the hanging effect. Glue to page and add word charm at top as a "hanger."

3. Cut 2" × 12" border from Cinnamon paper and glue down to background at left side. Add thin strip of Limeade over it. Place acrylic letters on the border. Once you have a visually pleasing spacing, peel the backing off the letters, one at a time, and stick them to the paper.

4. Print 2 photos of one image (here the mother and son). Use the 1" punch to cut the hands out of the second photo; glue that onto a round metal-rimmed vellum tag and adhere to the other photo with 3-D Glue Dots. This technique gives a raised effect and draws attention to important parts of photos.

5. Glue hinges to large picture of mother and son to give a solid feel.

6. Attach the matted poem beneath the large picture.

7. Glue Dot the metal heart plaque to the left of the poem.

From Your Scrap Stash...

Cardstock: Limeade, Flamingo, and white (Bazzill Basics)

Papers: "Aged & Confused" Sublime Collection Pack, 12" × 12" (BasicGrey)

Acrylic letters: Glass Effects, black, Imagine lowercase and Vintage upper- and lowercase, (Heidi Grace Designs)

Metals: metal-rimmed tags; Charmed Frames; square red brads; hinges; beaded chain; silver eyelets; photo slide frame; photo corners; Charmed Plaque with heart (Making Memories)

Scrappers Canvas for inkjet (Creative Imaginations)

PaperWare Stencil (Westrim Crafts)

Ribbon, blue sheer, ¼" (SEI)

Wood heart, ½"

CeramCoat acrylic paint, Napthol Crimson (Delta)

DuraClear Gloss Varnish (DecoArt)

Distress Ink, tea dye color (Ranger Industries)

Memory Book Glue Dots and 3-D Glue Dots (Glue Dots Int'l)

Paper trimmer (Fiskars)

1" and 1½" circle Jumbo punches (Marvy Uchida)

½" circle punch; ⅛" hole punch (EK Success)

Font: Artistic

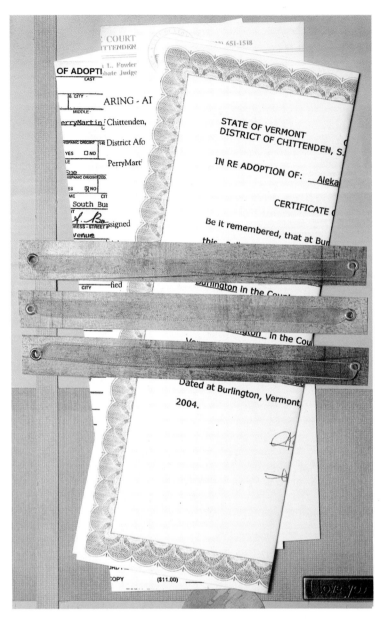

1. Repeat technique in Step 4 from Left Page with a photo of the child, punching out the face area and gluing on vellum tag.

2. Cut 3 strips of paper ½″ wide to hold documents; glue down at ends only. Put eyelets near ends of each strip and through the background. Thread the blue ribbon through eyelets and tape to back. Place the documents under the strips to hold them in place, then fan them out.

3. Place coordinating paper behind the "A" stencil and glue to back. Mat on white paper and apply metal-rimmed photo corners to 2 opposite corners. Glue to page.

4. Glue quarter with 3-D Glue Dot to 1″ square vellum tag backed with Flamingo cardstock; glue 3 small pictures on other tags. Arrange and glue to page.

5. Paint wood heart red and attach to Flamingo cardstock circle with a 3-D Glue Dot; "hang" chained charm from heart and glue circle and charm to page.

6. Glue matted journaling to page. Overlap photo from Step 1 with double-printed face and glue.

7. Arrange then attach "adoption day" letters along the bottom left.

8. Glue picture of sleeping baby behind metal frame, then glue to page at bottom right.

9. Punch holes and apply colored brads in open spaces on page to add texture and a pop of color.

10. Look at page and SMILE.

ACHIEVING A COLLAGE LOOK

Cut circles and strips of various widths from paper or cardstock, choosing colors that coordinate with your photos and back-grounds. Ink all paper edges for an aged look. Arrange the paper strips vertically and horizontally on the background to achieve a collage-like feel, adding the circles for contrast. I arrange several times before it feels right to me. Arrange matted photos over papers, moving papers as needed, until you get a design that feels balanced. Take a picture or trace positions, if necessary, to remember placement. Remove photos. Glue papers down, then glue photos in place. Add brads, charms, or other 3-D items to fill "holes" in the arrangement where a little something extra is needed.

First Day of Kindergarten

by Sue Eldred

Justin is the youngest of my three children. I'd sent his siblings off to kindergarten ten and fifteen years before, but it was so much harder on me to send him. The thought of this timid little guy riding a great big bus without me was tough. I'm not sure which one of us worried the most, but we got through it without any tears—his or mine. I rewarded him with a trip to his favorite restaurant, Chuck E. Cheese's. I've incorporated keepsakes from that first day at school, but I've also included a sketch of Justin, game tokens, and tickets from Chuck E. Cheese's. All this memorabilia is important in depicting Justin's big day!

...from the Memorabilia Box...

Name practice paper from school, bus-shaped name tag, child's artwork, photo sketch from restaurant, game tokens, tickets, prize

From Your
Scrap Stash...

To the Layout...

For Both Pages:

1. Choose 2 pieces of fun, school-themed background paper.

2. Trim photos, journaling, and keepsakes and mat or double mat with cardstock using tape runner.

Left Page:

1. Use tape runner to glue down writing practice sheet. Overlap double-matted child's photo and glue in place.

2. Make a chalkboard with a piece of black cardstock cut in a rectangle. Add thin strips of tan cardstock around the edges of the black; clip at 45° angles at the corners. Dab ink on the strips to age and stain them, giving the look of wood trim. Glue in place. Write on chalkboard with white colored pencil. Decorate with stickers.

3. Punch a mini file folder from buff-colored cardstock; score and fold. Write child's name on index tab. Print out "1st Day of School" and date on computer; cut out and glue in place on front of folder.

4. Make a scene using the school bus name tag. The road is torn gray cardstock glued onto a light blue background. Draw the lines for the road with a white colored pencil. Mat on gold cardstock.

5. Double mat school bus photo with red and gold.

6. Position all elements on page to achieve pleasing arrangement, then glue in place.

Right Page:

1. Try to use kids' original artwork as much as possible when creating their pages. Artwork really shows Justin's personality and lets him know how proud I am of his work. If the artwork is too big to fit on your page, you can have a reduced color copy made at your local copy center.

2. Journal on the computer and print out on white cardstock. Double mat with gold and green. Decorate with stickers.

3. Glue down keepsake photo/drawing, journaling, artwork, and prize.

4. Glue the tickets to a double mat of gold and green, at the lower right, adding special journaling.

5. For heavy items, such as the metal token, it's more secure to use a small clear envelope and glue it in place.

You never want to use that last token or all of your tickets. I wonder if you think that insures a return visit.

At the Zoo

by Carla Jacobsen

Sometimes you have to take a day or two to just get away from everyday life. My son, Cooper, and I took one such "mini-vacation" a couple of years ago and had a wonderful time together. Our destination: the Memphis Zoo. The brand new panda exhibit opened the day we went, and we were the among the first people to visit the pandas. We did have to wait in line, but along came a local reporter who took Cooper's picture and talked with us. The next day, that photo appeared in the newspaper—what a thrill for an eight-year-old!

...from the Memorabilia Box...

Newspaper article, panda exhibit tickets

To the Layout...

For Both Pages:

1. Use red cardstock for the backgrounds. Edge the cardstock with black ink pad, using a wiping motion, and allow to dry.

2. Print computer journaling on white cardstock sheets. Cut cardstock down to desired size, leaving open area at top for cut-out headline. Also edge this cardstock with black ink. Allow to dry.

3. Mat photos on cardstock and mulberry paper using Photo Tabs. Place Pop Dots underneath some photos to make them stand out. Do not adhere to the page at this point.

4. Cut stalks of "bamboo" from basswood about ⅛" to ¼" wide and various lengths. Daub walnut ink on them to give them a richer color. Allow to dry completely. Apply thin coat of rub-on gold with a cotton swab or foam applicator.

5. Cut various sizes of leaves—1" to 2" long—from basswood. Apply green rub-on to the leaves with a swab or foam applicator to achieve desired color. Adhere leaves to the bamboo stalk with glue. Allow to dry.

Left Page:

1. To create the hinged overlay newspaper article, follow these steps:

a. Scan newspaper article and print twice, once in color and once in grayscale. Use the grayscale article as your base paper. Cut the photo from the color copy and mat on black cardstock. Align photograph over grayscale picture and adhere.

b. Size the article to black cardstock, leaving approximately ⅛" on each side, but don't adhere. Just under the photo, cut the article horizontally. Adhere the bottom portion of the article to the cardstock.

c. The upper portion of the article will have hidden journaling beneath it. Mount the top of the article on another sheet of black cardstock with about ⅛" on the sides and top; adhere and trim so there is no black showing at the bottom, so the article overlaps the bottom portion exactly.

d. Put the brass hinges on the edge of the black cardstock/article top. Make holes in the paper with the piercer where the hinge holes are; attach the hinges to the top paper with mini brads.

e. Fold the unattached side of the hinges to the back side of the paper. Put in position over the blank black paper on the page. Carefully open like a book cover and pierce holes in the black and red cardstock underneath; attach the hinges to the background with mini brads.

f. Cut a piece of Java color cardstock almost as large as the black background; tear along one edge, for interest. Mat the "hidden" journaling on red, then on the Java. Attach the whole piece to the black cardstock.

g. Cut another piece of Java cardstock about ¾ the size of the black cardstock behind the newspaper article, tearing one edge. Adhere in place. Mat the sticker of the dragon on black then red; adhere to the center of the Java cardstock.

From Your Scrap Stash...

Cardstock: "Places We Love" Collection, 12" × 12" Bottle Glass Green (Bazzill); 12" × 12" Red Hot (2 sheets), Espresso, and Java; 8½" × 11" white, 2 sheets (KI Memories)

Paper: yellow mulberry (Paper Mojo)

Stickers: Jolee's Destination—Chinese Sticker Collage, dragon (EK Success); black letter stickers (Die Cuts With A View)

Metals: eyelets (Making Memories); brass hinges, label holder, and brads (Making Memories); Asian pendant by Elements (The Beadery Craft Products)

Basswood: 1/16" × 1" × 24" strip (Worldwood Industries)

Fibers (Fibers by the Yard)

Original EZ Walnut Ink with dauber tip (Fiber Scraps)

Adhesives: Pop Dots (Stamp Craft); Aleene's Quick Dry Tacky Glue (Duncan); Zig 2 Way Glue (EK Success); Photo Tabs (Fiskars); Xyron sticker maker (Xyron div. of Esselte)

Bamboo Clip (Altered Pages)

Memories black ink pad (Stewart Superior)

Metallic rub-ons, gold and green (Craf-T Products)

Tools: hammer, eyelet punch, paper piercer; and eyelet setter (Making Memories); 12" Personal Paper Trimmer and Self-healing Mat (Fiskars); X-Acto knife handle with No. 11 blade (Hunt Mfg.); Cutter Bee Scissors (EK Success)

Font: Bambino

h. Embellish the bamboo clip with fibers and then slide the clip just below the photo to create a little handle that will let the hinged flap open easily.

i. Adhere the newspaper article on the right-hand-side red cardstock, at an angle.

2. Position and glue down the mattted photo. Attach label holder and bamboo to cardstock with Tacky Glue.

3. Add stalks of bamboo to fill open areas.

Right Page:

1. Adhere journaling, leaving space at the top for the title.

2. Reverse print the title on back of Espresso cardstock; hand cut with craft knife. Run letters through Xyron, then apply gold rub-on to give them some sparkle. Peel letters from backing, and attach to page across white cardstock and background. Add black letters for subtitle.

3. Position and adhere matted photo-graphs to cardstock.

4. Adhere tickets to the page. Set eyelets on either side of the tickets. Loop fibers through the pendant and glue pendant to the tickets with Tacky Glue, then thread the fibers down through the eyelets and tie at back.

5. Add stalks of bamboo to fill open areas.

TOOL BOX:

For intricate shapes that are difficult to cut by hand, such as letters, try the Wishblade Personal Media Cutter. Wishblade connects to your personal computer like a printer and comes with its own software. It cuts shapes from ½˝ to 8˝ from cardstock, printed paper, vellum, and other media. Choose from fonts and shapes in the Wishblade Design Library or create your own images to cut, using your photos, clipart, or personal drawings.

Photo by Flexible Fotography, San Diego, CA

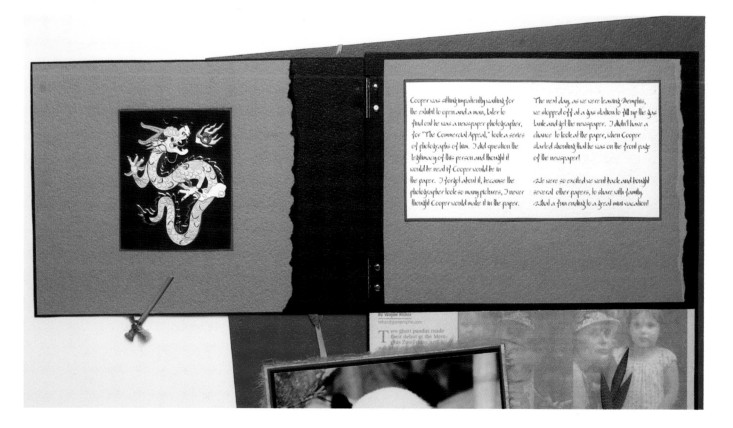

Family Pride

One of the basic human needs is to feel pride in our accomplishments. Honor your family by scrapping even small everyday accomplishments such as an A+ on spelling test. Of course, those ribbons for winning sporting events or school letters are more traditional representations of success. Make copies of those awards and honors or use the actual items for a dimensional addition to your albums.

Certificates of participation in volunteer work and membership pins also represent achievements. Any time your family members are mentioned in a newspaper article, even in the school or company newsletter, is cause for celebration with a scrap page.

Scouts and sports activities are an integral part of the lives of children these days, and it's a shame to relegate the reminders of those pastimes to shoeboxes. The pride of catching one's first fish or getting a Scout's cooking badge should be celebrated in a scrapbook. Another kind of pride is the reverence we have for those who are serving their country overseas; paper money, coins, postcards, flags, uniform patches, and letters are just some of the things you can use to accompany their photos in your album.

And let's not forget the ever-faithful members of our family, our pets. Reminders like collars, tags, or leashes help us celebrate their contribution to our family long after they are gone. Families should be the world's best support groups, and featuring awards, honors, and remembrances of accomplishments in our scrapbooks shows our pride in our family.

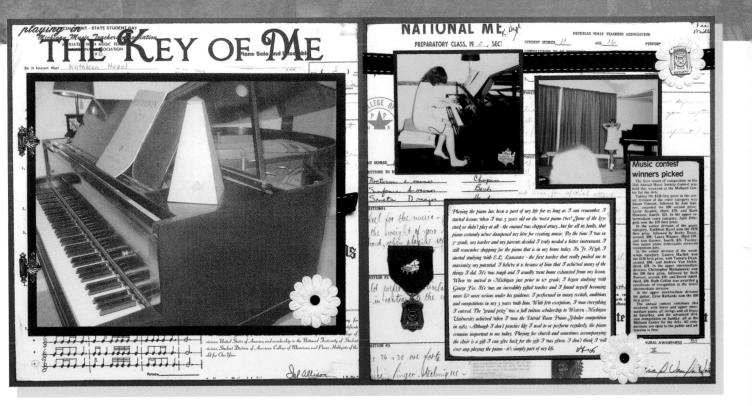

The Key of Me

by Kathe Cunningham

From a very young age, I participated in piano recitals, competitions, auditions…you name it! I saved every certificate, award, medal, and judge's comment sheet. Now, as an adult, I enjoy looking back at the comments and letters I received from judges and teachers. I have such a passion for making music and am thrilled that others were able to see that in my playing. That dedicated musician still lives in me—and now I can show future generations that part of me through my scrapbook pages as well.

…from the Memorabilia Box…

Judging forms, music, awards, medals, certificates, newspaper article

Music contest winners picked

The first round of competition in the 35th Annual Music Society Contest was held this weekend at the Midland Center for the Arts.

Taking the $120 first prize in the senior division of the voice category was Susan Vincent, followed by Ann Gurnee, awarded the $90 second prize; Leslie Graden, third, $70; and Barb Howison, fourth, $25. In the upper intermediate voice category, Julie Pillepich won the $70 first prize.

In the senior division of the piano category, Kathleen Hazel won the $120

From Your Scrap Stash...

Cardstock: Cardinal and Raven (Bazzill Basics); white (Paper Studio)

Ribbon: stitched grosgrain, Beetle Black (Doodlebug)

Flowers and buttons (Making Memories)

Stamp ink: StazOn, Jet Black (Tsukineko)

Chalk: red (Craf-T Products)

Computer fonts: Chocolate Box for title; Caslon540SwaD for journaling (1001 fonts)

Hinges: box closure, silver (7gypsies)

Printable canvas: Frederix Archival Inkjet Print Canvas (Tara Materials)

Special adhesives: Diamond Glaze (JudiKins); Glue Dots (Glue Dots Int'l); Dry Stick (RS Industrial)

To the Layout...
For Both Pages:

1. Scan several pieces of memorabilia. Using photo-editing software, merge scans into a single image. This will become custom patterned paper. Once merged, resize image to 11½" square.

2. Before printing, add title to paper using the software. Print completed patterned paper on white cardstock. Tip: If you do not have photo-editing software or a wide-format printer, you can achieve a very similar look with a photocopier at a copy shop. Use temporary adhesive to piece your memorabilia together and place on copier. Copy onto 11" × 14" paper, and trim to 11" square.

3. Repeat Steps 1 and 2 for a second sheet of custom paper, eliminating title step.

4. Ink edges of custom paper and adhere to Cardinal cardstock with glue stick.

Left Page:

1. Adhere one piece of memorabilia (I used a judge's evaluation sheet) to left page under title, leaving 1" between title and top of memorabilia.

2. Print 8" × 10" photo of piano on canvas. Trim edges, leaving no unprinted border. Mat photo with Raven cardstock, leaving approximately ¼" border on all sides.

3. Mount an additional piece of memorabilia (award certificate) on the back side of Raven cardstock.

4. Place matted photo on left page, covering previously placed memorabilia (from Step 3). Attach hinges using Diamond Glaze on left side.

5. Cut a 2" piece of ribbon. Fold in half and adhere using Glue Dots under the right side of the piano photo, lifting the edge slightly and sliding the ribbon underneath.

6. Chalk edges of 1 large and 1 small paper flower with red. Adhere the small flower to the large one and add a button center. Adhere to lower right corner of piano photo.

Playing the piano has been a part of my life for as long as I can remember. I started lessons when I was 5 years old on the worst piano ever! Some of the keys stuck or didn't play at all - the enamel was chipped away...but for all its faults, that piano certainly never dampened my love for creating music. By the time I was in 3rd grade, my teacher and my parents decided I truly needed a better instrument. I still remember shopping for the piano that is in my home today. In Jr. High, I started studying with E.L. Lancaster - the first teacher that really pushed me to maximize my potential. I believe it is because of him that I achieved many of the things I did. He was tough and I usually went home exhausted from my lesson. When we moved to Michigan just prior to 10th grade, I began studying with George Fee. He was an incredibly gifted teacher and I found myself becoming more & more serious under his guidance. I performed in many recitals, auditions and competitions in my 3 years with him. With few exceptions, I won everything I entered. The "grand prize" was a full tuition scholarship to Western Michigan University achieved when I won the David Bean Piano Scholar competition in 1982. Although I don't practice like I used to or perform regularly, the piano remains important to me today. Playing for church and sometimes accompanying the choir is a gift I can give back for the gift I was given. I don't think I will ever stop playing the piano - it's simply part of my life.

Right Page:

1. Mat 2 photos with Raven cardstock, leaving a ⅛″ border on all sides.

2. Mat newspaper clipping with Raven cardstock, leaving a ⅛″ border on all sides.

3. Computer generate journaling. Print on white cardstock and trim closely. Ink edges with ink pad.

4. Mat journaling block with Cardinal cardstock, leaving a ⅛″ border on all sides. Add second mat using Raven cardstock, leaving a very small border.

5. Place a piece of ribbon across top of right-hand page, leaving 1″ between top of ribbon and upper edge of page. Secure on back of page with glue stick.

6. Arrange photos, journaling block, and newspaper clipping. Adhere to layout.

7. Remove clasps from 4 medals and/or pins. Adhere one small pin to a medal. Attach securely to layout using Dry Stick. Adhere another small pin to upper left photo using Glue Dot or Dry Stick.

8. Chalk edges of all paper flowers using red chalk.

9. Adhere a small flower to the center of a large flower and add a black button center. Adhere completed flower to lower edge of journaling block.

10. Adhere final medal to center of last large flower. Adhere on upper right corner over ribbon.

Marines
The Few. The Proud.

Let Freedom Ring

by Patti Swoboda

Since the 2001 attack on the World Trade Center, many of us have friends and loved ones who have been deployed to the Middle East and other areas around the world to fight against terrorism. This project pays tribute to a single Marine serving in Iraq. It preserves items connected with his brave mission—a small American flag, a uniform patch, and Iraqi money, as well as photos—and becomes a time capsule to share with future generations. That Marine is my son, and I couldn't be more proud of him.

...from the Memorabilia Box...
American flag, uniform patch, foreign money

To the Layout...

For Both Pages:

1. On the back sides of 2 blue papers, use a ruler to measure 6½″ up and draw a line across. Use the line as a guide for tearing each sheet. (Optional: Use only 1 blue paper torn exactly in half.)

2. Line the straight edges of the torn sheets of blue paper along the bottom edges of 2 sheets of red paper. This will create the red and blue background for your layout. Important: Any photos you want partially beneath a blue torn edge need to be attached to the red before gluing the papers together.

3. Trace the bell pattern onto 2 sheets of translucent paper—one half on each sheet. Cut out the bell halves.

4. Place the top of each bell half at the top of a page and line its straight edge along the seam between the pages, so that the bell halves form a whole bell when the 2 pages are side by side. Do not glue yet.

5. Arrange stickers and photos on the pages as desired. Decide whether any photos or stickers are to be covered or partially covered by the translucent bell. Make sure you leave room for the page title.

6. Attach all stickers and photos that are to be under or partially under the bell. Use Xyron, a translucent paper-friendly adhesive, to attach the bell halves as instructed in Step 4.

7. Use the extra sheet of red paper to die-cut the page heading, "LET FREEDOM RING." As an alternative to die-cuts, you can stencil the letters, use alphabet stickers or rubber stamps, or handwrite the page title.

8. Place pages inside page protectors.

Left Page:

Place flag and patch memorabilia inside a 6″ × 12″ Page Flipper. Using the adhesive strip on the edge, adhere the Page Flipper to the left side of the page protector, *not* the page itself, unless you are not using page protectors.

Right Page:

Smaller Page Flippers were trimmed to fit the length of the Iraqi bills, then stacked one on top of the other, beginning with the largest bill on the bottom and ending with the smallest bill on top. Adhesive strips on each Page Flipper allow them to be stuck together at the top, then adhered to the page protector, so each bill can be lifted and viewed on both sides. If desired, Page Flippers may be adhered directly to the page when page protectors are not used.

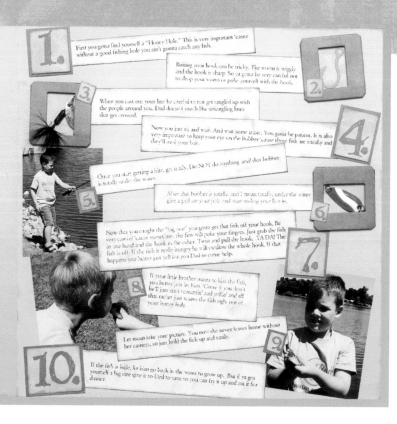

Lessons in Fishing

by Becky DeZarn

After a weekend camping trip, I overheard my oldest son instructing his little brother on how to catch the perfect fish. While listening to this conversation, I couldn't help but giggle. I decided I needed to write it all down to memorialize it on a scrapbook page. The journaling on these pages is quotations from my eight-year-old son. I wanted a rustic, camp-sign feel to the layout, and to achieve that look I used shades of brown and green and applied aging ink to all the edges. I raided his tackle box for a fishing lure and spinner to complete the authentic look.

...from the Memorabilia Box...

Fishing lure (without hook), fishing spinner

To the Layout...

For Both Pages:

1. Start with two 12″ × 12″ sheets of Dark Sand cardstock.

2. Lightly ink the cardstock edges by rubbing the Distress Ink pad on the paper.

Left Page:

1. Cut pieces of Light Sand cardstock 8½″ × 2½″ and 8½″ × 8″.

2. Stamp title on the 8½″ × 2½″ piece of cardstock and subtitle at the bottom of the 8½″ × 8″ piece. Ink the edges of the cardstock, dabbing ink in a random pattern to achieve a worn wood look.

3. Cut 2½″ × 1½″ and 1½″ × 1¼″ pieces from green canvas paper. Cut 1¼″ × 2″ and 1″ × 1″ pieces from tan texture paper. Layer the pieces and attach to opposite corners of your 4″ × 6″ vertical picture.

4. Attach picture with these corner embellishments to the 8½″ × 8″ piece of cardstock above the subtitle.

5. Attach 8½″ × 2½″ and 8½″ × 8″ pieces of cardstock to the 12″ × 12″ background cardstock, leaving ½″ between the 2 pieces.

6. To give the look of an old hinged sign, tie 2 photo anchors together with micro fiber. Repeat and then attach both "hinges" to the cardstock using Glue Dots.

7. Tie and knot micro fiber to 3 photo anchors. Attach to corner embellishments and photo using Glue Dots.

From Your Scrap Stash...

Cardstock: 2 sheets each Dark Sand, Light Sand, and Seal, 12″ × 12″ (Bazzill Basics)

Patterned Paper: Tan Texture and Green Canvas (Karen Foster Design)

Photo anchors, antique (Making Memories)

Slide mounts; micro fiber (Jest Charming)

Adhesives: Mini Glue Dots (Glue Dots Int'l); Pop Dots (Plaid Ent./All Night Media)

Tim Holtz Distress Ink; Walnut Stain (Ranger Ind.)

Stamps: large and small Four Score Titling (Purple Onion Designs)

Die-cut fishhook (QuicKutz)

Font: Garamond (Microsoft Word)

First you gotta find yourself a ... without a good fishing hole you ain't gonna catch any ...

Baiting your hook can be tricky. The w... and the hook is sharp. So ya gotta be ve... to drop your worm or poke yourself wi...

When you cast out your line be careful to not get tangled up with the people around you. Dad doesn't much like untangling lines that get crossed.

Now you just sit and wait. And wait some more. ... very important to keep your eye on the bobber 'c... they'll steal your bait.

Once you start getting a bite, get ready. Do NOT do anything until that is totally under the water.

After that bobber is totally, and I mean t... give a pull on your pole and start reeling

... you caught the "big one" you gotta get that fish off your ...

Right Page:

1. Print all journaling in areas of varying length on Light Sand cardstock. Cut the journaling apart in strips. Ink the edges of the strips, dabbing ink in a random pattern to achieve a worn wood look.

2. Assemble 3 shadow boxes by covering slide mounts with green canvas paper. Place Pop Dots on the back of covered slide mounts and attach to a 2″ × 2″ square of tan texture paper. Adhere memorabilia inside the shadow box using Glue Dots.

3. Stamp list numbers in various sizes on tan texture paper and lightly ink the edges. Mount number squares on green canvas paper.

4. Attach journaling strips, pictures, shadow boxes and numbers, overlapping and at odd angles.

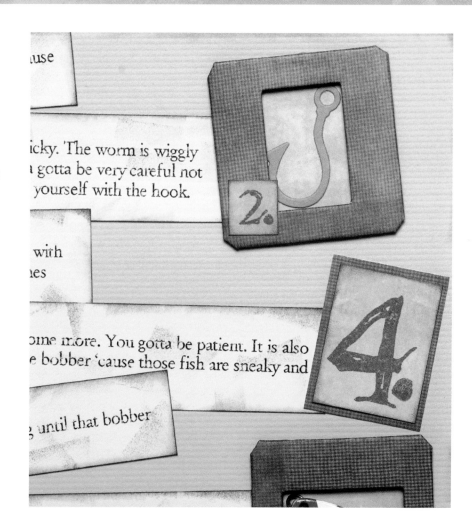

Scouting Ceremony

by Stacey Morgan

Being a part of Girl Scouts is such a rewarding experience. You get the chance to make new friends and learn new things with them. Girls work their way up in the program as they get older: first as Daisies, then Brownies, then Juniors, and finally Girl Scouts. A sash is a symbolic part of scouting, because it gives the girls a unique way to display badges they have earned trying new things. I've included my daughter's Brownie hat and sash in this layout, which she shows off with pride.

...from the Memorabilia Box...

Brownie sash and hat

From Your Scrap Stash...

Paper: Real Life Antique Light, 12″ × 12″, 2 sheets; Real Life Antique Dark, 12″ × 12″ (Pebbles, Inc.)

Cardstock: 8½″ × 11″, cream (The Paper Company/ANW Crestwood)

Patterned paper: The Mini Stack, sepia tone and daisy print, 6″ × 6″ (Die Cuts With a View)

Ribbon: Details, Antique Collection, bronze, about ⅜″ wide; cream, ¼″ wide; tan, ⅛″ wide (Making Memories)

Metals: Expression stencil phrase "All Girl"; rectangle zipper pulls, bronze, friends/laughter/enjoy (All My Memories)

Pen: fine-tip, brown (Creative Memories)

Font: LD Delightful (Lettering Delights)

Chalk: decorating chalks, tan and brown (Craf-T Products)

Adhesive: Mini Glue Dots and Pop-Up Glue Dots (Glue Dots Int'l); Fabri-Tac glue (Beacon Adhesives); Xyron 510 with Permanent Adhesive cartridge (Xyron)

To the Layout...

For Both Pages:

Trim the white edge off both sheets of Antique Light paper.

Left Page:

1. Prepare the sash: Position the sash to reach from corner to corner on the background page. You will need an extra ½″ of material that goes beyond the page edges; this will be folded over later when it is attached to the page. Cut the excess material off both ends, leaving only one thickness of material. Note: If the sash has badges on both sides, save the back to do another page. Run the sash through the Xyron machine to add adhesive to the back. Peel off the backing and adhere it to the Antique Light page, starting in the top left corner, leaving the extra ½″ of fabric extending beyond the page edges, then working down to the bottom right corner. Cut off the corner of fabric that extends beyond the page in a triangle. Fold the ½″ extra material to the back of the page. Repeat in the other corner.

2. Write your journaling on cream cardstock with a fine-tip brown marker. Trim the cardstock and apply tan and brown chalk with a cotton ball to the edges. Run through the Xyron machine to add adhesive and apply to a 6″ × 6″ daisy paper, off-center so the photo can overlap onto the paper. Apply Mini Glue Dots to the back side of the daisy paper and adhere it to the Antique Light paper, on top of the sash near the bottom right corner.

3. Mat the 4″ × 6″ photo in the bottom left corner with Antique Dark paper measuring 4½″ × 6½″. Run the matted photo through the Xyron machine and adhere to the Antique Light background paper, overlapping the daisy paper.

4. Crop 2 photos smaller for the upper right corner. To make the photo corners, run a 12″ piece of bronze ribbon through the Xyron machine. While still on the backing, cut into 1″ lengths. One at a time, place the center edge of the ribbon piece on the corner point of the photo. Fold the ends around to the back side. Repeat for each corner of the 2 photos. The remaining 4 pieces will be used for a photo on the other page. Run both photos with the ribbon corners through the Xyron machine and adhere to the to right corner of the page.

5. Tie a piece of ribbon through the "laughter" bronze zipper pull and adhere in the corner of the journaling box.

Right Page:

1. Prepare the hat: Cut away the back section of the hat so it will lie flatter and be less bulky. Leave about ½″ extra material on the sides of the hat to fold over to the back. Glue the extra material to the back side of the hat with Fabri-Tac glue; set aside to dry.

2. Crop a photo and adhere it off-center on a 6″ × 6″ piece of daisy paper. Run a 7″ piece of cream ribbon and a 7″ piece of tan ribbon through the Xyron machine. Adhere the cream ribbon to the bottom of the photo, across the daisy paper. Wrap the extra around the back. Apply the tan ribbon on top of the cream ribbon and wrap the extra over the edge. Tie a small bow with tan ribbon and adhere with a

Mini Glue Dot. Adhere the decorated daisy paper to the top left side of the page.

3. Apply Mini Glue Dots to the back of the "All Girl" bronze stencil phrase and place below the daisy paper on the background page.

4. Mat the 4″ × 6″ photo in the bottom left corner with Antique Dark paper measuring 4½″ × 6½″. Run the matted photo through the Xyron machine and adhere to the Antique Light background page.

5. Crop another small photo and make photo corners as described in Step 4 of the Left Page instructions. Run through

Xyron and attach to lower right corner of page. Tie a piece of ribbon through the "friends" zipper pull and place in the corner of the photo.

6. Type the Girl Scout Promise on the computer and print out in brown text color on cream cardstock. Trim the cardstock, chalk the edges with tan and brown, and mat with Antique Dark brown paper. Run through the Xyron machine and adhere to the page between the hat and photo.

7. Apply Pop-Up Glue Dots to the back of the hat and adhere to the upper right corner of the page.

Horsing Around

by Pam Archer

A young girl and her love for her horse can be a powerful combination. Throw in a local 4-H club to provide the training and opportunities for growth, and it yields an alliance that just gallops along…all the way to a state championship. Who knew she was just horsing around?

…from the Memorabilia Box…

Show ribbons, newspaper article, rosette (pin)

To the Layout...

For Both Pages:

Use the 2 "topstitched" pages for the backgrounds.

Left Page:

1. Cut a plain satin blue ribbon in half vertically. Position the blue ribbon's finished edge to extend ½" beyond the red show ribbon on both sides. Glue in place.

2. With pinking shears, trim the ribbons' upper and lower edges to a uniform length.

3. Glue the ribbon on the diagonal across the page, from left center to lower right-hand corner.

4. Make the felt photo frame by cutting these pieces: dark brown 6½" × 7½", tan 6" × 7", and light brown 5½" × 6½". Stack the felt largest to smallest (on top) with equal distances around the sides and pin together.

5. To create the saddle-stitched effect, use 3 strands of embroidery floss and backstitch through all 3 layers of felt, about ¼" in from the edge of the brown top layer. Tip: For very even stitching, machine baste around the frame. Then follow those stitches with your needle.

6. At the center of the felt, cut a rectangle to accommodate the photo.

7. Apply a second row of backstitching ¼" from the newly cut edge. Press the felt flat. Secure all corners by adding the Western-theme buttons. Center the picture in the frame, and glue the outer edges to the felt back.

8. Place the framed photo at the upper left, overlapping the ribbon. Lightly glue in place at the corners.

9. Using the brown foundation paper, trace around the die-cut spur. Glue the brown spur in place, on top of the die-cut, trimming out the hole. Moisten your finger with the embossing pad and transfer the embossing fluid to the "metal" part of the spur. Apply a coat of embossing powder and heat set. With your finger, fill in any empty areas by repeating the above. Glue the embossed spur on the page at the upper right.

10. Cut a 6" length of a photo strip. Using repositionable letters, spell out the horse's name on the strip. Center and glue it below the felt frame.

11. Load the horseshoe stamp with brown ink, and stamp 4 horseshoes on a second photo strip. Cut the prints into 1¼" lengths. Starting at the lower left-hand corner, alternate the horseshoes to simulate a walking pattern. Glue in place.

12. Carefully remove the horse from the die-cut rectangle. Save the square with the horse-shaped opening for the right page. Glue the die-cut on the faux leather piece, and trim the leather around the horse about ⅛" larger than the die-cut. Glue in place, overlapping the ribbons.

13. On a 6¼" length of photo strip, vertically spell out "Horsing Around." Glue the strip next to the ribbon's right edge.

From Your Scrap Stash...

Papers:
JoAnn's All-Occasion Scrap Book Kit, "topstitched" background pages, yellow and gold, 2 each; gold tag, 4" × 6"; Cardstock, aubergine; photo strips, 12", 2 (Jo-Ann Stores); brown foundation (Michaels); haystacks (Colorbök)

Fabrics:
Faux leather scrap, 6" × 8", dark brown; faux suede scrap, 6" × 9", cinnamon brown; felt squares, brown, tan, and dark brown

Threads and trims:
Embroidery floss, color #677 (DMC); Jewelry Designer, 1mm black leather cord and tan suede cord (Darice); blue satin ribbon, 2" wide, 12" long (Michaels)

Buttons:
⅝" cowboy hat, 2; ¾" cowboy boot, 2 (JHB Int'l)

Charms:
Hat and saddle (Charming Thoughts)

Die-cuts:
Tan Horse; spur (Michaels)

Stickers:
Alphabitties Rope Letters, repositionable (Provo Craft)

Stamps:
Little horseshoe; western cowboy hat and boot (PFY)

Ink pad:
Memories, brown (Stewart Superior)

Embossing supplies:
Embossing pad (Inkadinkado); embossing powder, Pearlustre, Garnet Opaque (Stampendous); Heat-It! gun (Ranger Ind.)

Glue:
The Ultimate (Crafter's Pick)

Stencils:
Ovals and circles (Creative Memories)

Small brad

Tools:
Straight paper scissors; decorative-edge scissors; hole punch; straight pins; crewel embroidery needle

Right Page:

1. Place the "County Fair"-type blue ribbon at the upper left-hand side. Glue in place. Add horse rosette (pin) at the top of the ribbon. Glue or pin in place.

2. Glue a 4½" × 6½" aubergine cardstock beside the ribbon, centered in the top half of the page.

3. With decorative scissors, cut the photocopied article's edges, leaving some white space at top and bottom. Glue the article over the left side of the aubergine cardstock.

4. Trim a small photo to 3" × 4". Cut a rectangle 3½" × 4½" from the haystack paper. Using the stencil, center an oval on the rectangle. Trace around the oval. Cut along the traced shape. Center the photo, right side up, in the oval frame. Glue in place at the lower right corner of the aubergine cardstock.

5. Load the hat and boot stamp with brown ink. Stamp the upper right-hand corner of the aubergine cardstock.

6. Cut a piece of faux suede 3" × 3¼". Glue the suede to the back of the rectangle that the horse die-cut was cut from. Glue in place beside the bottom of the ribbon.

7. Trim a small photo to a 2" square. Center the photo on the gold tag and glue in place.

8. Cut a rectangle 2" × 2¾" from the faux leather. Using the circle stencil, draw a 1½" circle on the wrong side of the leather. Cut out the circle. Position the leather frame on top of the photo and glue the edges in place.

9. Using the brown foundation paper, trace around the tag, adding ¼" to all sides. Place the gold tag on top of the brown paper, leaving a ¼" edge all around. Glue the tag in place. Punch a hole in the brown paper to line up with the hole in the gold tag.

10. Cut an 11" length of tan suede cord and fold in half. Slip the saddle charm on the cord, bringing the charm to the cord's center. Feed the open ends of the cord up through the tag's hole, then down through the looped end of the cord. Pull till tight at hole.

11. Glue the tag at the lower right of the page.

12. Cut a pair of chaps from the faux suede. To create the fringe, clip the outer sides ¼" deep every ⅛".

13. Place the chaps on the diagonal across the corner of the haystack-framed photo and glue in place. Add a small brad in the center.

14. To form the lariat, cut a 14" length of black leather cord. Place the cowboy hat charm in the center. Wrap the cord through the loop on the hat 4 times. At the top, wrap the cord ends around the lariat and knot several times. Apply a healthy amount of glue to the knot and place in the upper right corner.

tip

Stitched details on your pages lend a unique look and tactile element. Want to add a stitched edge to a photo mat, attach an interesting bit of fabric to a page, or stitch a die-cut to a greeting card? Just get out the Sew Crafty Mini Sewing Machine. About 6″ × 7″ × 4″, it runs on 4 AA batteries or an AC adapter accessory that's a must. The stitch on top is straight, with a chain stitch on the bottom, and practice makes perfect. Available from Provo Craft.

Photo by Flexible Fotography, San Diego, CA

Celebrating Our Dog

by Michaela Young-Mitchell

The layout celebrates the life of our dog, Bodie, who passed away last November. I included his collar and leash because they are symbolic of all the great trips and adventures we had with him. I chose to make it a celebratory layout, rather than a morose memorial layout, because I want to remember him with joy instead of sadness. The photos depict him in all kinds of environments, at various ages, and with various other family members (including our other dog). The journaling captures the highlights and memorable events of his time with us, focusing on the wonderful things about him. The only hint at his passing is on the engraved dog-bone tag (with his birth and death dates), and a bit in the journaling about his last walk.

...from the Memorabilia Box...

Engraved dog tag and well-used leash and collar

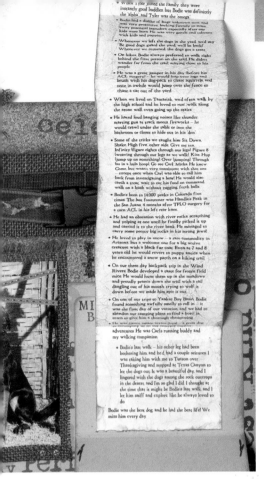

To the Layout...

For Both Pages:

1. Measure openings in cork tiles to fit collar and leash and flip book. Carefully cut windows with a craft knife and a metal-edge ruler.

2. Use red ink pad to color the outer tile edges and brown to shade the window edges.

3. Tie burlap strips and ribbon around window/tile edges.

4. Adhere burlap to back of tiles, behind desired openings.

5. Adhere brown cardstock to back of cork tiles.

Left Page:

1. Stamp title in red and black on cork tile.

2. Cut Pet Talk patterned paper about 6″ × 6″, ink the edges, and adhere to lower right of tile.

3. Adhere collar inside window with strong adhesive, then stitch onto background with embroidery floss to secure. Use Glue Dots to hold dog license tags in desired position.

4. Wrap ribbon around focal photo and tie on engraved dog tag.

5. Mat focal photo on burlap, fold bottom edge over bottom of photo, and secure with brads. Adhere to layout.

6. Print data onto front of file folder and stamp on file label.

7. Ink outer and inner edges of file folder with brown.

8. For journaling inside file folder, first crumple and iron inkjet paper. Print journaling from computer in 2 columns onto this paper. Cut paper in half and adhere the columns end to end to make one long journaling strip. Brush over the journal strip with brown chalk, then use red ink pad on edges. Fold accordion style to fit inside mini file folder, adhering the back of last page/panel to inside of file folder.

9. Adhere small photo and red cardstock strip to outside of file folder. Add mini brads to ends of cardstock strip.

10. Adhere file folder to layout over patterned paper. Use dog paper clip to hold file folder closed.

From Your Scrap Stash...

Cork tiles: ¼″ thick, 12″ × 12″, 2

Cardstock: Brownie; dark red (Bazzill Basics)

Papers: Pet Talk and Dog Bones (Karen Foster Design)

Metals: screw brads; mini screw brads; Alpha slides, antique brass; Paper Clip Pets (Karen Foster Design)

Burlap, deep red; Dog Poetry Stickers (Once Upon a Scribble)

Inkjet paper (Hewlett-Packard)

Decorating chalk, Kit #3 (Craf-T Products)

Ink pads: ColorBox chalk, Warm Red and Chestnut Brown (Clearsnap); VanDyke Brown (Ranger Ind.); Brilliance Black, Graphite Black (Tsukineko)

Letter stamps: Antique (PSX); Stencil (Ma Vinci's Reliquary)

Ribbon: brown (May Arts)

File folder (Rusty Pickle)

Embroidery floss to match collar (DMC)

Zig Writer pen (EK Success)

Adhesives: Easy-Stick Adhesive Roller (Henkel); Glue Dots and Glue Lines (Glue Dots Int'l); Memory Mount and Ultimate! glue (Crafter's Pick)

Tools: 12″ paper trimmer and ⅛″ hole punch (Fiskars); upholstery needle (Simplicity); craft knife; metal ruler; paper piercer

Font: Chestnuts (Two Peas in a Bucket)

Right Page:

1. Cut Pet Talk patterned paper about 5″ × 8″, ink the edges, and adhere to upper left of tile.

2. Cut leash to fit inside cork window. Hold the cut end over a match or candle to melt the nylon so it doesn't unravel. Adhere leash inside window with strong adhesive, then stitch onto background with embroidery floss to secure.

3. Mat large photo on red cardstock and adhere to layout over patterned paper.

4. Slide metal alphabet charms on leather strip. Punch ⅛″ holes in ends of strip, adhere over photo, and push mini brads through holes into cork background.

5. To make a flip book for lower left window: Cut Dog Bones patterned paper into 3½″ strips. Adhere 1¼″ wide red card-stock strip along center of pattern strips. Fold accordion style and adhere strips together to make flip book as long as desired. Cut brown cardstock to fit cover of flip book. Add stamped words and mini brads to hold flap of red cardstock. Ink cardstock edges and adhere over first page of flip book. Add photos and hand journaling to all pages of flip book. Adhere inside window in tile, gluing last page to burlap background.

6. Crumple and iron another piece of inkjet paper and chalk with brown. Place poem sticker on crumbled, chalked paper and trim to size. Ink edges in red. Adhere to cork background near center bottom of page.

7. Prepare another Alpha slide leather strip (as in Step 4) and attach across lower edge of poem.

Generations Long Ago

Only a few generations ago, photographs were very expensive and, as a result, very scarce. You may not have many photos of your great-grandparents when they were younger, but you can build a page commemorating them using memorabilia.

Letters and postcards from soldiers fighting World War I help future generations understand more about their lives. Special memorabilia such as Holy Communion ribbons and bits of trim or buttons from clothing are also some of the keepsakes with which you can scrap special pages.

Old jewelry, hairpins, eyeglasses, or even a well-used handwritten recipe card can bring back memories of grandmother. You can use the originals or make copies to use in your layouts. Well-used small tools, membership cards, licenses—all these images can be incorporated in your historic albums.

If you are short on memorabilia from your ancestors, look for items that date to their era. Check thrift shops for almanacs from notable years. Your local library will have books with images that bring the past to life. And don't forget to journal information from those who knew the person or stories about him or her.

What a treasure! The wartime diary of Tommy's grandfather, Felixe Honore, is a most fascinating account of his experiences as a part of the American Expeditionary Forces, both stateside and in the war-ravaged country of France. His descriptive musings give us a revealing look into the personality of the man in the doughboy uniform and the role he played in "The Great War". Although his diary ends with the armistice, it was at this time that his real journeys began as he was given the position of French interpreter for the major. As he traveled throughout France with his superior, selling the surplus livestock to the people of the country, he collected postcards from the various cities and towns. On the back of one such card he wrote, "I saw this with my own eyes. You should get an album and keep all these cards for souvenirs." Indeed we have!

Over There

by Madeline Fox

As a soldier of the American Expeditionary Forces, my husband's grandfather, Felixe Honore, kept an incredible record of his journey through the French countryside at the end of World War I. His journal full of amusing anecdotes and serious observations, a handful of picture postcards with his unique commentary on the back, and a photograph of him in his military uniform served as the basis for these pages, titled "Over There—Felixe in France."

...from the Memorabilia Box...

Copies of WWI journaling, antique postcards

From Your Scrap Stash...

Cardstock: Cardinal and Raven (Bazzill Basics); white (Paper Studio)

Ribbon: stitched grosgrain, Beetle Black (Doodlebug)

Flowers and buttons (Making Memories)

Stamp ink: StazOn, Jet Black (Tsukineko)

Chalk: red (Craf-T Products)

Computer fonts: Chocolate Box for title; Caslon540SwaD for journaling (1001 Fonts)

Hinges: box closure, silver (7gypsies)

Printable canvas: Frederix Archival Inkjet Print Canvas (Tara Materials)

Special adhesives: Diamond Glaze (JudiKins); Glue Dots (Glue Dots Int'l); Dry Stick (RS Industrial)

To the Layout...

For Both Pages:

1. Cut and tear patterned papers, arranging and adhering on cardstock base, to create background as shown in photo of completed project.

2. With fleur-de-lis stamp and gold paint, randomly decorate background.

3. Scan old photographs, vintage postcards, or other ephemera and reprint for use on the page and in the pocket if the actual items will not be used.

4. Mount photographs on black cardstock, Sonnets patterned paper, then black cardstock again.

5. Punch out the letters for the jigsaw alphabet title. Use the positive letter shapes except for the H, which uses the negative stencil. Paint with 2 coats of white acrylic. When dry, sand edges and give a light wash of walnut ink. Let dry again. Attach fleur-de-lis eyelet to letter "O." Tie ribbons to edge of letter "H" stencil and back with black-and-white patterned paper. Adhere title letters along the top, spanning the 2 pages of the layout.

Left Page:

1. Use alphabet stamps to add a subtitle underneath the title letters on the left-hand page.

2. Cut a piece of patterned paper for the pocket, approximately 4″ × 8″, folding edges underneath. Adhere bottom and sides to background.

3. Print journaling, distress edges with ink, and adhere to front of pocket.

4. Fill pocket with actual or duplicated ephemera. For this page, postcard backs and fronts were scanned and included. Blank pages of the actual journal were scanned and journal entries were reprinted. Several of these journal pages were joined with a jump ring and embellished with ribbon before being added to the pocket.

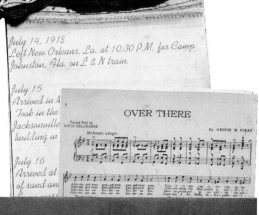

July 14, 1918
Left New Orleans, La. at 10:30 P.M. for Camp
Johnston, Fla. on L & N train.

July 15
Arrived in N
Took in the
Jacksonville
building in

July 16
Arrived at
of sand an

OVER THERE

French Text by
LOUIS DELAMARRE

By GEORGE M. COHAN

Moderato allegro

JOURNAL

What a treasure! The wartime diary of Tommy's grandfather, Felixe Honore, is a most fascinating account of his experiences as a part of the American Expeditionary Forces, both stateside and in the war-ravaged country of France. His descriptive musings give us a revealing look into the personality of the man in the doughboy uniform and the role he played in "The Great War". Although his diary ends with the armistice, it was at this time that his real journeys began as he was given the position of French interpreter for the major. As he traveled throughout France with his superior, selling the surplus livestock to the people of the country, he collected postcards from the various cities and towns. On the back of one such card he wrote, "I saw this with my own eyes. You should get an album and keep all these cards for souvenirs." Indeed we have!

Right Page:

1. Adhere double-matted photo to page at left under title.

2. Mount 2 postcards on black cardstock, add photo corners, and adhere to right side of page.

Credit: Duke University Historic American Sheet Music archives, a project of the Digital Scriptorium Rare Book, Manuscript, and Special Collections, http://scriptorium.lib.duke.edu/sheetmusic/. Note: Images of these music pieces, all dating to prior to 1920, can be used freely as long as proper credit is given to the website.

JOURNAL

What a treasure! The wartime diary of Tommy's grandfather, Felixe Honore, is a most fascinating account of his experiences as a part of the American Expeditionary Forces, both stateside and in the war-ravaged country of France. His descriptive musings give us a revealing look into the personality of the man in the doughboy uniform and the role he played in "The Great War". Although his diary ends with the armistice, it was at this time that his real journeys began as he was given the position of French interpreter for the major. As he traveled throughout France with his superior, selling the surplus livestock to the people of the country, he collected postcards from the various cities and towns. On the back of one such card he wrote, "I saw this with my own eyes. You should get an album and keep all these cards for souvenirs." Indeed we have!

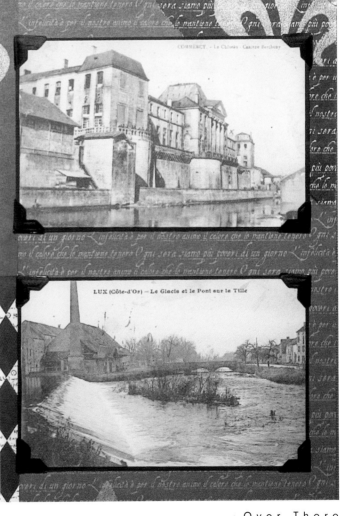

Our Gang

by Elaina Pecora

Photographs are amazing. They can take us back to times gone by, and they can open the gates to other memories. In my father-in-law's family album, I found wonderful pictures of him and his family as children. In some of the photos, I saw a remarkable resemblance to the child stars of the film series *Little Rascals*. Then, while rummaging through some old boxes, I found several decaying pieces of fabrics and was able to connect them to some of the pictures I had found. The result is this family layout going back to 1905, combined with the comedies of my childhood—*Little Rascals* and *Our Gang* of the 1940's.

...from the Memorabilia Box...

Ribbons, fabric swatches, buttons

To the Layout...
For Both Pages:

1. Make a textured border of mulberry paper on the outside edge of each sheet of sepia paper. Cut a 4″ × 24″ sheet of light brown mulberry paper—strips may be glued together to create 24″ length. Scrunch paper into a tight ball. Straighten paper out slightly. Apply a 2″ border of glue to one side of each background paper. Scrunch the 4″ × 24″ paper into the 2″ × 12″ glued area. Paper can easily be manipulated. Make a 2″ × 24″ strip of beige mulberry paper—scrunch, open, and glue on top of brown paper.

2. Border all sides of sepia papers with decorative gold paper trim, creating a straight edge on scrunched paper. Vary designs used to create interest.

3. Select photos and memorabilia that help tell the story of your layout. Make copies of your pictures on good-quality photo paper. To maintain the tone of the original pictures, it may be necessary to apply stamp pad ink to the edges and surface of your pictures. To create a worn look, rip edges or fold some of your picture copies and apply stamp ink to the torn edges.

4. Label pages by gluing fabric tags to scrunched border of each page. Use Collage Alphabet to print your title on the tags.

Left Page:

1. Glue top of Communion ribbon and one tail on page. Glue related photo to partially cover ribbon at right side of page.

2. Put stick pin in another photo and glue at left, partially covering top of ribbon.

3. Lay tail of ribbon with printing on it over one corner of photo and glue in place.

4. Mount photo for lower right on corrugated paper with a strip of tan mulberry paper glued near the top. Add clip at top of photo. Glue in place, overlapping tails of ribbon slightly.

5. Add additional titling using Sticko letters on the sepia page.

6. Use rub-on designs to add interest to page edges, corners, or blank spaces.

7. Print names of people in photos on vellum. Glue on or near pictures.

8. Glue Dot camera on page at upper right.

It can be difficult to apply glue to fragile memorabilia such as fabrics and ribbons, and you need an overall application of adhesive to maintain the integrity of the piece. For best results, use acid-free spray adhesive on the back or run the piece through a Xyron machine. Then you can carefully place it on your layout without damaging it.

From Your Scrap Stash...

Papers: Then and Now, sepia linen, 12″ × 12″, 2 sheets (American Traditional Designs); mulberry paper, beige and light brown; light tan corrugated paper (DMD Ind.); vellum paper, white

Embellishments: accordion book, black; Li'l Frames, World Travel Collection, 4; Li'l Clip, Then and Now Collection; rub-on design sheets, Then and Now Collection and Family Collection (American Traditional Designs); Nostalgiques, Rebecca Sower Designs; fabric tags, Remnants Collection; stick pin; fabric ribbon and tag closures; Tag Types Sticko letters (EK Success)

Lettering: Life's Journey Collage Alphabet (K & Co.)

Adhesives: The Ultimate! glue (Crafter's Pick); Photo Glue Stick (Pioneer); Glue Lines and Glue Dots (Glue Dots Int'l)

Ink pad: Van Dyke Brown (Ranger Ind.)

Right Page:

1. Remove back cover of accordion book to help eliminate some bulk. Edge the inside pages of the book with stitched ribbon on top and bottom. Add pictures. Tear mulberry paper almost as large as cover. Journal on vellum paper and tear out. Glue mulberry and vellum papers onto accordion book cover. Glue back panel to upper right of sepia page.

2. Mount photos on corrugated and mulberry paper as shown. Tear mulberry paper slightly larger than the picture. Use decorative trim, buttons, and gold paper trim on and around pictures and accordion book to pull everything together visually.

3. Use pictures from public domain websites or purchased prints of film star look-alikes to form a connective theme between your picture memorabilia and journaling. Trim to size of metal film frame and glue from behind. Use dimensional dots and lines adhesives to adhere film frame embellishments to family pictures.

4. Glue open frame to cover of accordion book, then add camera charm to inside of frame.

5. Remember to identify photos, using computer-printed vellum.

Poppy Ben was born in 1905 and Grandma Josephine was born in 1907. "Poppy" was born on the Lower East Side of Manhattan, under the Brooklyn Bridge- "The Bowery".

Poppy and his friends thought who they were! Everyone was going to gain fame through boxing. After Poppy Ben's first professional fight, he retired-he didn't like to get hit.

Poppy and his friends always reminded me of the Bowery Boys (aka. East Side Kids). They even looked like them.

Bowery Boys

by Elaina Pecora

My father-in-law, Benedict Pecora, grew up on the Lower East Side of Manhattan near the New York side of the Brooklyn Bridge in an area known as the Bowery. The kids who grew up in that rough neighborhood frequently planned to make their fortune as boxers and bore a striking resemblance to film characters in the *Bowery Boys*, also known as the *East Side Kids*. Benedict felt he could be the next champ and spent a great deal of time in the gym. His mother was very upset with his decision, but to no avail. The big night came—his first professional fight. When he was quickly knocked out, it convinced him he wanted to work for the railroad.

...from the Memorabilia Box...

Old film, 1929 almanac, beige ribbon and trim

From Your Scrap Stash...

To the Layout...
For Both Pages:

1. Attach ribbon or trim to right sides of 2 earth-tone paper sheets for background pages.

2. Using images taken from a public domain website, enlarge images and print in black on white paper. Adhere to the background pages, piecing together as needed to cover most of background.

3. Flatten bottle caps by sandwiching them between 2 pieces of wood and hammering. Add adhesive letters to inside of bottle cap for your title. Glue bottle tops to right-hand side of both sheets of paper, overlapping ribbon or trim.

4. Select pictures and memorabilia to tell your story. If you don't wish to use the original photos, copy or scan and print them onto white cardstock.

Left Page:

1. Tear page from almanac. Glue to page at upper right on an angle. Add watch design clip to top corner.

2. Mount 2 photos on corrugated paper, using photo corners on 2 opposite corners. Glue over background photo.

3. Use photo corners to attach another photo over the almanac page.

4. Print journaling on vellum. Trim and mount using photo corners on earth-tone paper cut about ¼″ larger than the journaling all around. Adhere at lower right over background photo.

tips

SHAKER BOX PHOTO KEEPERS

Another way to hold multiple photos is to slide them into a large shaker box. Just leave off one of the strips on the back and attach the box to the page with the open side up. Insert photos, either on a ribbon string or individually. The first photo can be seen through the window on the box.

Right Page:

1. Create a "video box" from ⅛" thick foam board. Cut one 3" × 5" rectangle, two ¼" × 5" strips, and one ¼" × 2½" strip. Adhere narrow strips to side and bottom of rectangle, creating a pocket. Cut old image to 3" × 5" and glue to top. Paint all sides black.

2. Cut several pictures to fit inside the box. Attach the pictures together vertically to a length of ribbon, leaving a loop at the top and about 4" of ribbon between the photos, so that the pictures can be placed in the box accordion style. Insert the pictures in the box, gluing the bottom end of the ribbon inside and leaving the tab sticking out. Apply glue to ¼" strips on back of box and adhere to background.

3. Mount remaining pictures on corrugated paper using photo mounts. Adhere pictures to background.

4. Attach filmstrip to background with Glue Dots. Take end of film around pictures and box, attaching here and there with Glue Dots.

5. Print journaling on vellum. Trim and mount using photo corners on earth-tone paper cut about ¼" larger than the journaling all around. Adhere over box photo.

The Family Business

by Michele Emerson-Roberts

Charles Frank Roberts was born in Texas in 1912, the eleventh of twelve children in a really "dirt poor" family—the floors of their home were actually dirt. He knew that the only way to leave that bleak life was to get an education, so he studied hard and worked odd jobs to help his family and pay for his schooling. Finally Charles became an optometrist, married, and had two children. His son, Charles Ray, joined the optometry practice in 1965, and granddaughter Cheryl came to work there a few months before "Papa" passed away in 1998. The family business goes on as Papa dreamed it would.

...from the Memorabilia Box...

Old optometric tool, antique eyeglasses, license, certificates, other old documents

To the Layout...

For Both Pages:

1. Scan the license, certificates, and other original old documents. Reduce and enlarge the items to obtain various sizes. Print on several sheets of heavy white paper or cardstock, printing more sheets than you think you will need—extras can be used for other projects. Also scan and print photos if you do not want to use the originals.

2. Reserve several small sizes of each document copy to mat and use as focus pieces later. Tear around the edges of these miniature documents, laying the ruler edge just outside the document and pulling the excess paper up and against the edge of the ruler to create slightly feathered edges on the papers. Set aside.

3. Tear the rest of the copies in random sizes and shapes, tearing some pieces freehand and others against the edge of the ruler.

Photo by Flexible Fotography, San Diego, CA

Arrange the torn papers in a pleasing collage, overlapping and turning the pieces in various directions, then glue them to one of the 12″ × 12″ white cardstocks.

Photo by Flexible Fotography, San Diego, CA

Repeat this process for the second sheet, or copy the first sheet if you want an exact match. Allow to dry.

4. To determine the layout, lay unmatted focus pieces onto each of the collage pages along with the photos, allowing ⅜″ to ½″ all around each piece as space for the triple matting. If you have too many pieces, delete some or make accordion books to hold more. Then place 3-D pieces overlapping or near the documents. When you have a pleasing arrangement, remove the photos and documents one at a time and triple mat them: first on black, about ⅛″ larger than the photo or document on each side, then on Sauterne, about ⅛″ to ¼″ larger than the black, and finally on black again, about ¹⁄₁₆″ larger than the Sauterne on all sides. As you finish matting each piece, lay it in position on the 11¾″ × 11¾″ pieces of foam board.

5. When everything is in place on the foam boards, draw a rectangle around each area that will hold a 3-D object, allowing a small space around the matted documents in that same area. Remove your matted and 3-D pieces from the foam board, laying them on your work-table in the same positions that they will be glued onto the background later.

6. Place the cutting mat under the foam board and cut the niche with the craft knife, discarding the piece you cut out. Repeat for the other page.

7. Glue the collaged paper onto the front of each of the foam boards with the niches in them. Turn the foam board over so you can see through the niche to the back of the collaged paper. Use the ruler and pencil to draw an "X" in the niche, connecting the opposite corners of the niche. Lay the foam board on the cutting mat and cut the X through the collaged paper.

8. Fold the flaps created by the X cut to the back of the foam boards, and glue in place. Cut off any excess paper that extends beyond the foam board.

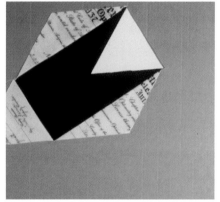

Photo by Flexible Fotography, San Diego, CA

Left Page:

1. Glue another piece of collaged paper to a piece of white cardstock. Cut to size about 2″ larger than the niche. Glue to the back of the foam board, so the collage shows through the niche at the front.

2. Glue 11¾″ × 11¾″ chipboard or cardboard to the back of the foam board.

3. Place the adapters on the Stylus handles and put the Fluid Chalk Cat's Eye pads onto the adapters. Gently apply ink around the outside edges of the niche and the page, alternating colors.

4. Glue 3 matted pieces in the niche.

5. Lay the antique tool in the niche over the matted pieces. Use the push pin to make 4 holes in the matted pieces all the way through the chipboard backing: 2 holes on each side of the vertical holder near the center and 2 near the top. Fold a piece of silver wire in half and put one of the open ends on each side of the vertical holder near the middle, then take each end of the wire down through the holes made with the push pin. Pull through and twist the wire ends together at the back. Repeat near the end of the holder, twisting the wire ends at the back. Cut off excess wire.

6. Glue additional matted certificate and photo in place on right side of page.

Right Page:

1. Glue the matted receipt to a piece of cardstock 2″ larger than the niche for the glasses. Glue to the back of the foam board, so the receipt shows through the niche. Let dry.

2. Glue 11¾″ × 11¾″ chipboard or cardboard to the back of the foam board.

3. Place the adapters on the Stylus handles and put the Fluid Chalk Cat's Eye pads onto the adapters. Gently apply ink around the outside edges of the niche and the page, alternating colors.

4. Place the glasses in the niche and make 6 tiny holes with the push pin to mark where the wire will be—2 on opposite sides of each hinge where the side pieces meet the eye glass, and 2 more in the center where the folded side pieces meet. Fold a piece of wire in half and put the open ends on each side of the hinge area, then take each end of the wire down through the holes made by the push pin. Twist together at the back and cut off excess wire. Repeat for the other end of the glasses and at the center of the side pieces.

5. Glue matted certificates, photos, and information about the family member in place on the background.

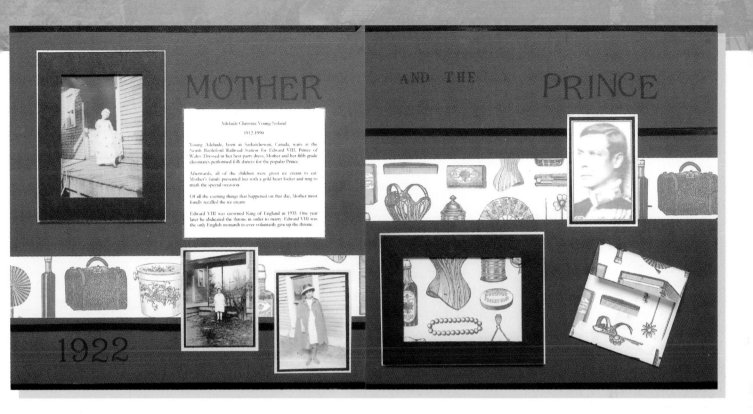

Once in a Lifetime

by Catherine Mace

My mother, Adelaide, was born and raised in Canada. The highlight of her childhood came in 1923 when she and her fifth-grade classmates performed folk dances for Edward VIII, the popular Prince of Wales. Afterward her family presented her with a gold locket and ring in commemoration of the event. In 1936, Edward VIII was crowned King of England, but later that year, in order to marry an American divorcé, he abdicated his office—the only English monarch to ever voluntarily give up the throne.

...from the Memorabilia Box...
Locket and child's ring

From Your Scrap Stash...

Mi-Teintes paper, burgundy, 12″ × 12″, 2 sheets; Mi-Teintes paper, black, ¼″ × 12″, 6 strips (Canson)

Other papers, cards, and templates: Rossi Italian prints, "Ladies Fashion," 1 large sheet; rectangular die-cut cards with solid back, black, 2; cardstock, black; square envelope template; text-weight paper, gold metallic; accordion card, 6-panel, 3″ × 18″, black; Italian Bakri book paper, Everest White, 8½″ × 11″ (Papers by Catherine)

Adhesives: acid-free glue stick (Tombow); Incredibly Tacky glue (Crafter's Pick); red-liner double-sided tape (Therm O Web)

Stamps and ink: alphabet rubberstamps set (Hero Arts); pigment ink pad, black (Tsukineko)

Acetate window plastic, 4″ × 5″ (JudiKins)

Clear matte photo corners (Xyron)

Heavy black railroad board or museum board, 100% rag or cotton-fiber (fine art or hobby stores)

Tools: pencil; scissors; craft knife; cutting mat; hole punch; large soft brush; bone folder

Font: Book Antiqua

To the Layout...

For Both Pages:

1. Cut Rossi "Ladies Fashion" paper into 2 strips, each 2″ × 12″. Adhere to 12″ × 12″ burgundy Mi-Teintes paper, positioned as shown in photo.

2. Attach strips of black Mi-Teintes paper to top and bottom of both pages using glue stick. Add additional strips above and below Fashion paper strips, as shown.

3. Mount small photos on gold metallic paper and black card stock, leaving about a ⅛″ to ¼″ border of each color around the photo.

4. Arrange individual elements on pages and move assembly around until a pleasing design is achieved, but do not adhere yet. Use rubber stamp alphabets to stamp all words and date on pages.

Left Page:

1. To make the raised photo frame: Glue or tape main photo (at least 4¼″ × 3″) inside black die-cut card, and adhere front frame of card to back. Mount card on gold metallic paper about ¹⁄₁₆″ larger than the card. From black railroad or museum board, cut 4 strips measuring 5¼″ × ½″ and 4 strips measuring 3″ × ½″. (As an alternative, use strips of black foam core board cut to the same lengths, 2 of each size.) Using a very sharp blade and craft knife, make several cuts through the thick board, rather than trying to cut through all at once. Glue or tape 2 strips of the same size together, creating a total of 4″ stacks, which will be used to raise the card off the background. Use red-liner tape or tacky glue to attach stacks to back of card. Adhere the longer stacks first, then the shorter ones, placing them almost at the edge of the frames. Glue on page at upper left.

2. Print out journaling on Italian book paper. Mount on page with clear photo corners.

3. Adhere 2 smaller matted photos to page, overlapping Fashion paper strip.

The Abdication Speech of Edward VIII

December 11, 1936

of my life, only upon the single thought of what would, in the end, be best for all.

This decision has been made less difficult to me by the sure knowledge that my brother, with his long training in the public affairs of this country and with his fine qualities, will be able to take my place forthwith without interruption or injury to the life and progress of the empire. And he has one matchless blessing, enjoyed by so many of you, and not bestowed on me: a happy home with his wife and children.

During these hard days I have been comforted by her Majesty my mother and by my family.

Right Page:

1. With a pencil, trace smallest square envelope template on wrong side of Fashion paper. Cut out with scissors, and following instructions on template, score on fold lines using end of bone folder. Fold left flap over right, and glue; fold up bottom flap and glue in place.

2. Print out text or journaling for accordion card on white book paper with a line length of no more than 2½". Cut apart into 6 panels, each 2¾" square. Use glue stick to adhere one printed panel to each panel of accordion card. Print out a title panel and mount on gold metallic paper, then glue to front of accordion card.

3. Slip folded accordion card into square envelope you made, and set aside.

4. To make the memorabilia box: Cut back flap off a black die-cut frame card. Cover one side of the card back with Fashion paper and punch 2 holes about ½" down from the top edge and about 3½" apart. Run ends of necklace chain through holes and tape down tightly on back, after adjusting necklace locket to fall near center of card. Use red-liner tape to adhere acetate window plastic to black frame. From black railroad or museum board, cut 4 strips 5¼" × ½" and 4 strips 3" × ½". (As an alternative, use single pieces of black foam core board cut to the same lengths.) Using a very sharp blade and craft knife, make several cuts through the thick board, rather than trying to cut through all at once. Glue or tape 2 strips of the same size together, creating a total of 4" stacks for the memorabilia box, 2 long stacks and 2 shorter stacks. The stacks will create the box effect, acting as spacers between the frame front and Fashion paper back. Use red-liner tape or tacky glue to attach stacks on back of die-cut black frame—the same side to which you taped the acetate window. Adhere the longer stacks first, then the shorter ones, placing them almost at the edge of the frames. Clean the inside of the acetate window with a soft brush. Put tacky glue or tape on the backs of the spacer stacks and attach frame to card back so necklace is framed in opening. Mount memorabilia box on gold metallic paper about 1/16" larger than the box all around. Glue mounted box on page.

STAMPING TITLES

To stamp the words for your title near the top of a page, turn the page upside down, so the top is right under your eyes. This way, you do not have to reach across the page and risk smearing ink on the background paper. Also, it's much easier to line up the letters. Lay a ruler across the page and use it as a guide for the placement of your stamps. Of course, it's best to practice first on scrap paper, which also gives you a clear indication of where to place the title on the page.

Note: Memorabilia boxes and raised photo frames on facing pages should be placed so they do not touch each other when the album is closed.

5. Adhere photo and accordion card envelope to page.

The ministers of the crown, and in particular, Mr. Baldwin, the Prime Minister, have always treated me with full consideration. There has never been any constitutional difference between me and them, and between me and Parliament. Bred in the constitutional tradition by my father, I should never have allowed any such issue to arise.

Ever since I was Prince of Wales, and later on when I occupied the throne, I have been treated with the greatest kindness by all classes of the people wherever I have lived or journeyed throughout the empire. For that, I am very grateful.

I now quit altogether public affairs and I lay down my burden. It may be some time before I return to my native land, but I shall always follow the fortunes of the British race and empire with profound interest, and if at any time in the future I can be found of service to His Majesty in a private station, I shall not fail.

And now, we all have a new King. I wish him and you, his people, happiness and prosperity with all my heart. God bless you all! God save the King!"

Vacations and Holidays

If there is anything that inspires us to collect memorabilia and bring it home, it is the family vacation. We want to grasp onto every moment and take it back with us to savor. What better place to keep these memories but our scrapbooks.

Paper money and coins make interesting additions; you can photocopy them in various sizes and collage them until they cover entire page backgrounds. Of course, there are the inevitable postcards from our stops along the way—be sure to buy interesting stamps to post them with and send some to yourself with on-the-spot journaling. Matchbook covers, paper menus, tickets to tourist attractions, and boarding passes for the airline all can help to tell the story of your trips.

Copy the stamps in your passport to add to your pages. Cut out elements from travel guides, tourist brochures, and maps. Even receipts for purchases, pages from foreign language dictionaries, and local crafts such as handmade lace can add interest to your pages.

Remember, holidays are like mini-vacations. Tell the story through tangible bits of the event: fabric swatches from Halloween costumes, children's artwork, paper decorations, and other distinctive pieces of memorabilia help you relate your family traditions for celebrating the holidays.

Great Vacation

by Sharon Mann

One of the highlights of my life was traveling to Italy to visit my daughter Shawna, who was attending school in Florence. We toured Rome, Florence, and Venice, wandering the cobble-stone streets, shopping, sightseeing, and eating delicious meals. I was enthralled by the colors, the textures, the food, the romantic language, and the people of Italy. These pages represent my Italian vacation memories: a "road" travels through the pages, map pieces highlight the cities, the papers and fabric are reminiscent of Italy. I've even written simple phrases in Italian and given the pages an Italian title…Great Vacation! "Divertiti!" Have fun making your own vacation pages.

…from the Memorabilia Box…

Menu, map, paper money and coins, museum tickets, postage stamps, matchbook

To the Layout...

For Both Pages:

1. Cut two 12″ × 12″ black mat boards to use as pages.

2. Draw a curving "road" with wavy edges on the Latte cobblestone paper, which will extend across both pages, varying from about 6″ at left to 3″ at right. Using a dry brush technique (dip in paint, then wipe almost all off on a paper towel), brush across the cobblestone to leave a bit of color; alternate red and stucco colors to give more dimension. Cut out using deckle-edge scissors. Lay this road on Espresso cobblestone paper; cut another layer of road, about ¼″ to ½″ wider than the original, with deckle scissors.

3. Cut out paper shapes and use 3-D paint for lettering and border, as seen in the "Rome" oval. Also, add 3-D paint lettering on some pictures and postcards. Set aside to dry.

4. Tear and cut coordinating papers to use as backgrounds: mix and match 4 or 5 coordinating colors of paper for a collage effect. Use maps (at top of pages) or menus (at lower right) from your travels as backgrounds, as well. On the map, circle the areas traveled and highlight with colored pencils. Attach this layer of background papers to the mat boards using paper glue or double-sided scrapbooking tape. The road goes on last, overlapping the papers; adhere the larger road first, then the smaller on top. The black mat boards should be completely covered.

5. Run a line of tacky glue where some of the papers meet, and lay ribbon or fibers in the glue.

6. Title: For each letter, cut a 1½″ square of fabric. Cut a 1″ square from scrap cardboard. Lay the fabric on your work surface in a diamond shape; place the cardboard square over it, with the corners of the fabric sticking out from the sides of the cardboard. Fold the 4 corners of fabric to center back of cardboard, and attach with tacky glue. Lay stencil letter on front of fabric-wrapped cardboard and apply Texture Magic over the opening with a palette knife to create a dimensional letter on the fabric. Remove stencil. Repeat for all letters of title. Let dry. Use Zots to attach letters to collaged background.

7. Page borders: Glue a fancy yarn or trim to the outside edges of both pages. To finish, glue a charm or button front in each corner with tacky glue.

From Your Scrap Stash...

Paper: Paper Palette Neutrals Collage Pad (Provo Craft); Sonnets by Sharon Soneff, Historical Scrapbook Collection, Terra Cotta, Near East, Fleur de Lis, Plum & Moss, Dark Moss Wash (Creative Imaginations); Cobblestone, Chai Latte, and Double Espresso (FiberMark)

Mat board, black (Crescent Cardboard)

Scrap cardboard pieces

Embellishments: Light Topaz Bead Mix (Blue Moon Beads); Crystal Innovations and Designer Metal Sliders (Pure Allure);

Charming Embellishments Bon Voyage Charms (Darice); Metallic Basics Mini Circle Brads (Making Memories); ScrapEssentials, Bright Star Brads (Jo-Ann Stores)

Fibers: fabric scraps; embroidery floss; crocheted doilies; ribbon; lace; yarn

Paints: Texture Magic Spring Green and palette knife from tool set; Ceramcoat Tuscan Red and Roman Stucco (Delta); Scribbles 3-Dimensional Paint, Iridescent Copper (Duncan)

Stencil Mania Happy Alphabet (Delta)

Adhesives: A Fine Line liquid glue and Premier Glue Stick (Adhesive Tech); Scotch Scrapbooking Tape (3M); Aleene's Original Tacky Glue (Duncan); 3-D Memory Zots, ½″ dia. (Therm O Web)

Photo corners, beige (Canson)

Tools: decorative border scissors, deckle (Provo Craft); beading needle; embroidery needle; embroidery hoop; scissors; craft knife; small flat paintbrush; colored pencils, white and orange; oval and circle templates; beading needle

Left Page:

1. Envelopes with interesting postmarks and stamps can be used to hold several pictures, as in the center of this page. Tear or cut envelope from top to bottom in a jagged line, slightly smaller than the photos. Attach a charm and painted destination label to the envelope front. Add paper pull tabs to ends of photos with descriptions of pictures.

2. Embroidered letters: Draw letters on fabric by hand, or use stencil or rub-on letters as a guide. Embroider letters on fabric using a simple satin stitch. Use the template to draw a circle around each letter. Thread beads on wire or fine thread till they extend around the circle; couch (stitch down) in several places around the circle with thread, or glue beads in place with Fine Line glue. Cut out stitched fabric circle at least ¼" larger than the bead circle; glue to cardstock circle for stability, then attach along the edge of the road using a Zot.

3. Fabric wrapped frame: Cut a 2½" × 3" piece of cardboard. Measure in ½" from the edges, draw another rectangle, and cut out to form frame. Trace around outer and inner edges of frame on piece of fabric. Place in embroidery hoop and embroider the frame between the 2 lines, adding beads here and there. Cut out fab-

ric about ½" larger than outside of frame. In center rectangle, cut diagonally, connecting opposite corners to form a cut "X". Lay embroidered fabric face down, then put cardboard frame over it, with the X cut in the center. Wrap the center fabric points around to the back of the cardboard; trim excess fabric points and glue to cardboard. Cut a triangular point of fabric off each corner on the outside of the frame. Fold each side of fabric to back, and glue to cardboard. Glue the photo to the cardboard back, so it shows through the frame opening. Use Zots to adhere to scrapbook page, overlapping road and envelope.

4. Adhere paper money and coins to ribbon on left side of page. Put a bit of lace or crochet underneath a coin to highlight it.

Right Page:

1. Picture pockets (lower left): Measure the pictures to go into the pockets. Cut piece of cardstock, adding an additional inch on the 2 sides. (Example: If picture is 4" × 6", make cardstock 6" × 6".) Fold

the paper under ¼" on the sides and bottom, so pocket is at least ½" wider than the pictures to be inserted. Cut or tear the top opening creatively: curved, diagonal, or straight across. Add brads to the corners, put glue or tape on the back flaps, and adhere to the page. Decorate the pocket with ink, lace, buttons, brads, or charms. To identify photos, use 3-D paint to label them, add eyelet and fiber with tag, or glue on pull tabs with descriptions.

2. The picture pocket under the title was made to hold horizontal photos. Cut cardstock 5" × 7"; fold back ½" tabs on one end, top, and bottom; and hold in place with brads at corners. Apply glue or tape to the back of these flaps and attach to page. Use photo corners to put photo or postcard on front of pocket. Add lace or paper tab to end of photos to use as a pull tab.

3. Glue bits of lace, charms, buttons, fibers and a matchbook on page. Handwrite foreign phrases directly on page or on paper cut in a banner shape.

Studying Abroad

by Linda Turner Griepentrog

In October 1989, I did something that few Americans had done before—visit the Soviet Union before its dissolution in 1991. The trip was organized by People-to-People International to promote international understanding and friendship. The highlight of the trip for me, as editor of the magazine *Sew News,* was meeting a counterpart, Luba, the fashion editor at a women's magazine called *Rabotnitsa.* We proudly exchanged our respective issues. I spent the rest of my free time shopping at fabric and notions stores, and visiting the GUM department store.

...from the Memorabilia Box...

Travel log, receipts, coins, paper money, brochures,
collector's pins, sewing patterns, handmade lace

To the Layout...

For Both Pages:

1. If you have original memorabilia you don't want to actually attach to the layout or that is too bulky or heavy, scan or copy it to get a paper version. I made duplicates of the photos, paper money, coins, passport cover, nesting doll, watch face, and more, by scanning; then I resized the items as needed to fit the layout.

2. Use black paper for the backgrounds.

Left Page:

1. Glue the red bookmarks in place at the left side of the page. Overlap passport cover copy and tourist brochure and adhere. Use brads to hold vellum quote in place overlapping the bookmarks and passport cover.

2. Punch out a star and cut a hammer and sickle from a scrap of yellow paper or cardstock and glue to top bookmark. Tip: Symbols like these, as well as flags, can often be found on tourist brochures when you are traveling.

3. Glue back of slide mounts to grosgrain ribbon; allow to dry before attaching the collector's pins in the center of each. Glue to page.

4. Glue lace piece to top of page, trimming off excess.

5. Arrange receipts, travel log, paper money copies, and so on, overlapping in a collage near the center of the page. Add copies of stamps, coins, doll, and other small items over the top.

6. Glue on plane charm and small journaling block.

From Your Scrap Stash...

Paper or cardstock: yellow scrap; white; corduroy, black, 12″ × 12″, 2 sheets (The Paper Co./ANW Crestwood)

Bookmarks: The Write Stock, red, 2 (The Paper Co./ANW Crestwood)

Decorative-edge scissors (Fiskars)

Glue: The Ultimate! (Crafter's Pick)

Inkjet printable fabric (Printed Treasures)

Mini brads (Galloping Horse Productions)

Metals: passport/travel log, Life's Journey Travel Log (K & Co.); plane and scissors charms and colored safety pins (Darice); brads

Slide mounts, varied colors (Magic Scraps)

Paper Shapers star punch (EK Success)

Ribbon: grosgrain, black, 1½″ wide, and tape measure (Offray)

Quote Stacks vellum quote, Travel (Die Cuts With A View)

Роботнитса

Роботнитса (Robotneetsa) magazine, the equivalent of Woman's Day in the U.S., hosted our People-to-People International group in October, 1989.

Луба (Luba), the fashion/sewing editor, and I became friends as she created a dress for me, using only string to measure and scissors to cut. Few Russian patterns exist, so she used her string and drew on the fabric to cut the garment, while we all watched in awe.

Her antiquated machine and serger hummed, and within the hour the dress was ready and it fit! Though not a style I'd wear at home, I do treasure it for the memory of my Russian friend and author of several sewing books.

Sewing's pretty much the same the world 'round--it's all about fabric and passion!

Right Page:

1. String the scissors, and glue at spots across page.

2. Glue pattern fronts and instructions at top left of page.

3. Trim scanned fabric with decorative scissors to about 3″ × 9″. Glue at upper right, over end of string.

4. Type journaling into the computer and print on white cardstock; trim to size and overlay the scanned fabric.

5. Add photos, tape measure, and safety pins.

6. Tear the fabric around the printed words, fringe the edges, and hold in place on the page with mini brads.

Family Travels

by Susan I. Jones

Our family trip to London was a once-in-a-lifetime experience for us. We gathered memorabilia to represent the visual richness of this historic city, including images of historically important people, places, and objects. We also collected postcards, books, papers, brochures, and even candy-bar wrappers with interesting graphics. Collages composed of these images showcase these memorabilia on my scrapbook pages. Family photographs complete the theme "Pussy cat, pussy cat, where have you been? I've been to London to look at the Queen."

...from the Memorabilia Box...

Decorative papers, reproduction maps,
copyright-free images of English queens

To the Layout...

For Both Pages:

1. Use ZipDry paper glue to adhere decorative paper to each 12″ × 12″ piece of cardstock for the base scrapbook pages.

2. Tear out paper images for the outer corners of the scrapbook pages. Use a makeup sponge to apply caramel color stamping ink to "age" the torn edges.

3. Run the torn and inked corner images through the Xyron or apply paper glue. Adhere the paper pieces in place on the outer corners of the 2-page spread.

4. Use a foam brush to apply Tea Dye Varnish to both pages. Set pages aside to dry.

5. Select images for collages of queens. Photocopy each image onto glossy photo paper. Cut out the images with craft scissors, cropping as desired. Glue a patterned background on cardstock, then arrange the photocopied images on top to compose a collage. When you are satisfied with the composition of the collage, glue down the individual overlapping pieces. Repeat for second page collage.

6. Photocopy the completed collages. To obtain contrast, copy colored collages in the printer's black-and-white mode. Keep originals to use in other projects.

7. Apply a coat of Tea Dye Varnish to photocopies if desired. Let dry, then glue collages in place on the scrapbook pages.

8. Use your sewing machine to frame the corner motifs and collages with free-motion stitching to add texture to the pages. Caution: Too much stitching will overperforate and weaken the papers.

9. Stamp and emboss with gold around the edges of the collage. Take care to aim the heat gun away from the collage or mask it off temporarily with a piece of cardstock to protect the photocopied collage.

10. Further embellish edges and stitching around collage with gold paint pen. Glue gold paper doily pieces and motifs to create a "frame" area around the collage. Add faux jewels to frame elements with dots of glitter glue. Set aside to dry.

11. Print out family photos onto glossy photocopy paper. Cut out, compose, and glue down 2 groups of photos. Select additional photos to be used separately on the page.

12. Scan and print family photo compositions onto inkjet canvas to add a textural dimension. Enrich the colors of the canvas photos with oil pencils or colored pencils. Glue canvas photo compositions to cardstock or poster board.

13. Cut out photo groups using an X-Acto knife on a cutting mat. Make a slight gold border around each group of photos using a gold leafing pen.

From Your Scrap Stash...

Cardstock: 12″ × 12″, 2 sheets each for page base; several sheets, white

Decorative paper: 2 sheets 12″ × 12″, for page background (I used printed papers and reproduction maps purchased in a gift shop, but you can get fancy printed papers from Papers by Catherine in their Italian, Japanese, and Indian lines.)

Adhesive: Zip Dry paper glue (Beacon Adhesives); Xyron 510 Create-a-Sticker with permanent adhesive cartridge (Xyron)

Paper Plus Tea Dye Varnish (Delta)

Adirondack Dye Ink stamp pad, caramel; embossing stamp pad and powder, gold (Ranger Ind.)

Rubber stamp: Crown-Ornamentum (Uptown Design)

Inkjet media: Fredrix Archival Print Canvas, Desktop Inkjet Canvas, 8½″ × 11″ (Tara Materials); Premium Plus Photo Paper, high gloss, inkjet, 8½″ × 11″; Premium Inkjet Paper, 8½″ × 11″ (Hewlett- Packard)

18kt gold leafing pen (Krylon)

Prismacolor pencils (Sanford Corp.)

ColorBox MetaleXtra Pigment ink stamp pad, GoldRush (Clearsnap)

Paper doilies (HyGloss)

Gold paper motifs, stars (ARTchix Studio)

Stickles glitter glue, magenta (Ranger Ind.)

Page Pebbles large clear circles (Making Memories)

Tools: X-Acto knife and blades (Hunt Mfg.); cutting mat; embossing heat gun; sewing machine with size 14 or 16 jeans/denim needle and gold metallic thread for machine stitching (Superior Threads); craft scissors (Fiskars); 1″ foam paintbrush; foam makeup wedges

14. Make slide mechanisms with the group photos as indicated below. Glue completed photo slide mechanisms in place on scrapbook pages. After glue dries, check the slides to ensure a smooth operation. Add Page Pebbles to the back of the photo groups for support if needed. The smooth surfaces won't interfere with the sliding action.

15. Add any additional canvas photos and journaling to complete the scrapbook pages.

16. Finish the edges of the completed scrapbook pages with a gold marker or ink pad.

Making Slide Mechanisms

Construct sliding mounts using scraps of cardstock or poster board and glue for photo groups as shown. Make 1 assembly for each photo group you want to slide across the scrapbook page.

1. **Base and spacers:** Use cardstock or poster board to make a rectangle the width and length appropriate for the space on your scrapbook page. Cut out 2 of these rectangles with an X-Acto knife on a cutting mat. Glue decorative paper to the front side of each rectangle.

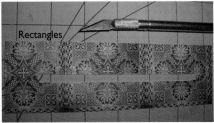

Photo by Susan I. Jones

2. **Base with slot:** Decide whether you want a straight track or a wavy one. Draw the sliding track on the back of 1 of the rectangles. Make the track approximately ¼″ wide between the parallel lines. Cut out the track between the drawn lines using an X-Acto knife on a cutting mat.

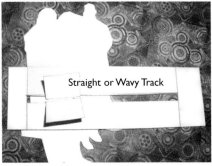

Photo by Susan I. Jones

3. **Slide mechanism:** Cut a strip of cardstock or poster board 1″ × 5″. Fold the strip as shown.

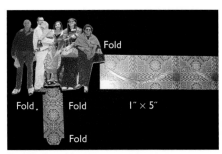

Photo by Susan I. Jones

Apply glue where indicated on the folded strip. Glue strip to back of family photo group.

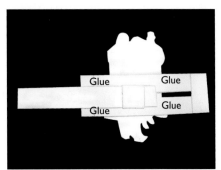

Photo by Susan I. Jones

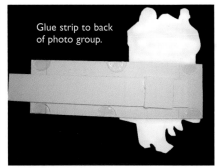

Photo by Susan I. Jones

4. **Lever:** From the front of the rectangle, insert the slide mechanism into the track. Working from the back of the photo and slide track, cut Page Pebbles in half and glue to the rectangle as shown. This allows room for the slider to slip easily along the track.

Photo by Susan I. Jones

Cut a strip of cardstock or poster board approximately twice the length of the rectangles. Glue decorative paper to the front of this strip. Glue the lever to the folded surface of the slide mechanism as shown. Cut a piece of cardstock or poster board 1″ × 1″ and glue over joins.

Photo by Susan I. Jones

tip

FREE-MOTION MACHINE EMBROIDERY TIPS:

Use a sewing machine in good working order with a fresh needle. For metallic threads, use a size 14 or 16 jeans/denim needle. Loosen the top tension on the machine, and bypass the last thread carrier above the needle if necessary to avoid abrading or shredding the metallic thread. Use a regular thread in the bobbin. Drop the feed dogs and bring the presser foot lever to the darning or embroidery position. Consult your sewing machine manual for additional details, if needed.

Be sure the photo group moves easily along the track.

5. Stop: Make a stop to prevent the photo group and sliding mechanism from escaping the sliding track. Cut a ½″ wide × length of lever strip of cardstock or poster board that will glue onto the photo group just above the slide mechanism and slip behind the rectangle with the track. Glue the end of this strip to the back of the lever under the rectangle. Trim strip as required.

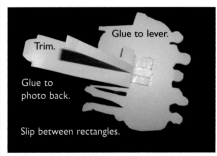

Photo by Susan I. Jones

6. Finished mechanism: Glue the slotted rectangle with the photo group to the backing rectangle. Apply the glue to the surfaces of the backing rectangle that the lever bypasses as it slides along the track.

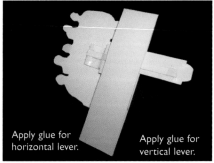

Apply glue for horizontal lever.

Apply glue for vertical lever.

Photo by Susan I. Jones

tip

COLLAGE CONSTRUCTION NOTES:

For collaging, you may want to use photocopies of your memorabilia instead of the originals. Print several copies of each image, in both black-and-white and color, for options in composing your collages. Use features on the copier such as reducing, enlarging, reversing the image, and color or black-and-white as you build your collages and make additional design decisions. After gluing your design together, you can photocopy your completed collages to use on the final pages, preserving the originals and giving less weight to the pages.

Spooky Fun

by Annette Bailey

Each year friends and family are invited to our house for a Halloween get-together. It's a stress-free holiday that's nothing but pure fun and make-believe. Kids, and even some of the adults, dress up in costumes and enjoy a weenie roast, tractor rides, ghost stories, crafts, games, and lots of sugar! Every fall I sew new costumes for my children and sometimes for nieces, nephews, and friends' children. Fabric scraps are clipped and collected in a pocket and showcased along with photos in this scrapbook layout, so the kids in my life will never forget.

...from the Memorabilia Box...

Fabric swatches from old costumes, ribbons, buttons, and foam candy corn decoration

To the Layout...

For Both Pages:

1. Choose some large photos and several shots that can be cropped smaller for the accordion foldouts. Note: Any photos that will be featured in the accordions may have embellishments touching them that may not be archival quality. If this is of concern, use scans or make sure you have duplicates of the chosen photos.

2. Use 2 Halloween-print cardstocks for page backgrounds.

Left Page:

1. To make a backing for the title, cut a 2¾" × 11¼" rectangle of orange cardstock. Tear a piece the same size from the orange sheer paper. Place on the cardstock and hold in place with adhesive dots.

2. Place the precut metal letters on top of the cardstock/sheer, and adhere with colored brads or eyelets attached all the way through the background.

From Your Scrap Stash...

3. Choose a contrasting color of cardstock, and stamp the letters "f", "u", "n." Cut around the letters and glue in the metal frames. Apply the frames to the cardstock/sheer rectangle.

4. Cut a 5" × 12" strip of white cardstock. Create an accordion fold with 4 sections. Glue two 18" lengths of sheer ribbon to the back of the accordion card one-third of the way from the bottom; the ribbon ends should extend equally from each side of the accordion.

5. Fold accordion, mat feature photo in center of black cardstock with room on both sides for decorating, and glue to the front panel of the accordion. Use the glitter glue with fine-tip writer to spell out the word "Magic" to the right of the photo. Cover it in fine glitter, dump off excess, and let dry. Coat a small cardstock scrap with a thin layer of glue, apply glitter, and dump off excess. Let dry, then punch out small stars and glue them to the left of the photos. Let dry.

6. Fold open the accordion and choose photos to fit inside. Mat, if desired, and glue in place. Journal on contrasting cardstock. Add desired embellishments: ribbons, buttons, punched stars, painted backgrounds, small stamped Halloween motifs, and glitter paint. Let dry well before folding, then close and tie a bow with the ribbons to keep it in place.

Henry reads ghost stories
(fit for kids of course!)

Ghosts & Goblins
howlin' good time!

Ben and Jake
compete in the
mummy wrap game!

Jackson plays ring-toss
on the spider's legs.

The kids get ready.

Cardstock: Halloween patterned, 12" × 12", 2 sheets; black; coordinating solids

Paper: vellum, white, 2 sheets; vellum, pale green; handmade sheer paper, orange

Ribbon: 3 coordinating colors of ⅛" to ¼" wide sheer, 1 yard each

Die-cut or stencil: Pumpkin (about 2" × 3")

Metals: Eyelet Letters to spell out title word "spooky"; metal frames, 1" × 1¼", 3; colored wire, thin gauge, 6" (Making

Memories); colored eyelets and setting tool or brads

Clear memorabilia pocket, 3½" × 4"

Rubber stamps: alphabet; Halloween motifs (Paper Inspirations); metallic ink stamp pad (Stewart Superior)

Glitter: fine glitter and glitter glue with writing tip (Art Institute Glitter); glitter spray; glitter paint

Orange seed beads

Scrap of acetate or clear page protector

Foam mounting tape

Embellishments: Jolee's Boutique paper motifs: witch's hat, spell book, wand, and pumpkin; Jolee's Boutique dimensional stick-on pom-pom spiders, 8 (EK Success); small charm "treats" tag (Doodlebug); wiggle eyes; tiny mirrors; trim; tag

Paint: metallic or flat in colors to coordinate

Adhesives: Glue Dots, Glue Lines (Glue Dots Int'l); photo-safe glue stick; paper glue stick

Tools: small star punch; paper trimmer; decorative-edge scissors

7. Invitation tag: Invite each guest to the Halloween party with a special scrapped tag, then use one tag to journal the page. Use a 3½″ × 5½″ black cardstock and cut the top at angles to form the tag. Spray the tag front with glitter. Let dry. Apply an eyelet to the top of the tag, and tie in ribbons. Print out, "Wanted: Ghosts & Goblins for a howlin' good time" and the party information on cardstock, and glue to front and back of tag, respectively. Make a shaker box using a pumpkin die-cut or stencil and cutting out the pumpkin center. Cut acetate to outer pumpkin shape and adhere with Glue Lines to the back of the pumpkin. Place ¼″ strips of foam tape on the back of the acetate all around the perimeter of the pumpkin. Sprinkle beads, snips of sheer paper, and glitter on the acetate inside the foam tape. Turn tag front over on top of the foam tape and press firmly in place. Add a die-cut or hand-cut leaf. Note: Because it is a single layer, these tags can be placed in a regular-sized envelope and mailed to your guests.

8. Mat 2 photos on cardstock and glue, overlapping, under title. Glue tag to lower left and accordion of photos to lower right using adhesive dots.

Right Page:

1. Cut two 2¼″ × 12″ strips of black cardstock. Create 2 accordion folds with 4 sections each; overlap one section at the end of each strip and glue them together to make one long strip. Choose photos, crop to fit the spaces, and glue in place. Choose embellishments to fill the remaining pages: large wiggle eyes, small mirrors, stamps, appropriate paper motifs, glitter, and so on.

2. Overlap 3 die-cut pumpkins at the lower right of the page and glue in place. (Alternative: Use stencil and trace 3 over-lapping pumpkin shapes on orange cardstock.)

3. Print out large journaling block on white vellum. Place over the pumpkins and use brads to hold the vellum in place.

4. Add a ready-made paper motif such as a witch's hat to the left side. Use glue stick to adhere.

5. Crop the larger photos as desired and back with a mix of coordinating cardstock and vellum. Adhere the photos with Glue Lines or photo-safe glue stick. Tip: Choosing different mat textures adds more interest to the layout.

6. Arrange the photos like the sample or use your own arrangement. Group smaller photos together by using a solid-color mat behind them. Use clear adhesive dots to affix the photos to the pages.

7. Attach the black accordion foldout using adhesive dots to secure it to the green vellum at the third photo place on the strip. Thread a 6″ length of colored wire under the cardstock between the adhesive dots. Lightly twist together at the front and add a charm, such as "treats." This will allow access to unfold the accordion paper, but will keep it in place on your page.

8. Place the fabric swatches and candy corn decoration in a clear memorabilia pocket, and adhere to the center top of the page.

9. Place the pom-pom spiders on the pages here and there to draw the viewer's eye around the layout.

Thanksgiving Feast

by Wendy McKeehan

Some things that our children make are kept by moms everywhere. I am quite sure that handprints of any kind are among those keepsakes. The majority of craft items that come home from school, club meetings, and parties get thrown away—the sheer volume requires it—but I could never bear to discard any of my children's handprints. One good example is these turkeys made in kindergarten by tracing my daughter's hands. They are the perfect accompaniment to this cute picture taken during the Thanksgiving-week festivities in class.

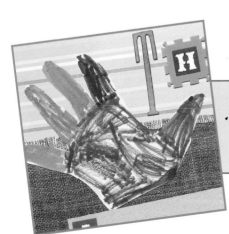

...from the Memorabilia Box...

Handprint turkeys on marker-colored paper

To the Layout...

For Both Pages:

1. Start with 2 pieces of plain cardstock for background (this will not show).

2. Cut two 4″ strips from each of the stripe papers.

3. Cut one 12″ × 12″ piece of brown fabric in half and fray the 12″ edges.

4. Attach the stripe papers at the top and bottom of both pages, alternating the types, then add the fabric to the center of the background using double-sided Scotch tape.

5. Color the chipboard letters with walnut ink and let dry.

6. Use the rub-ons to spell out your title on the foam shapes.

7. Adhere the title of jigsaw letters and foam shapes to the page.

8. Attach brown and red foam shape "leftovers" to the opposite corners of the layout.

Left Page:

1. Print out journaling on buff cardstock, omitting the first letter and indenting the text. Rub a letter sticker of the first letter on a foam square and glue it to the beginning of the journaling.

2. Attach ribbons to back of journal block at upper right corner. Glue foam shape corner to lower left of journaling block. Glue block in place, overlapping fabric and striped paper.

3. Glue handprint turkeys in place.

Right Page:

1. Mount photo on buff cardstock and attach various short lengths of ribbon to the bottom. Glue foam shape corners to upper right of photo mat.

2. Add rub-on date, vertically, to the lower right corner.

From Your Scrap Stash...

Scrapperware Connectiles foam shapes; Impress-Ons letter stickers; Artistic Scrapper hemp fabric, 12″ × 12″, cocoa color (Creative Imaginations)

Stripe papers, 12″ × 12″, 2 sheets (Scenic Route Paper Co.)

Cardstock: buff color

Jigsaw alphabet letters "T", "S", and "F" (Making Memories)

Ribbons, assorted colors and prints (May Arts)

Herma Vario tab dispenser (EK Success)

Scotch double-sided tape (3M)

Original E-Z Walnut Ink with dauber top (Fiber Scraps)

Font: Pure Imagination (Two Peas in a Bucket)

I think that it is a Kindergarten right of passage to make handprint turkeys the week before Thanksgiving. Tori was so excited to show me the turkeys and of course, like any good Mother would, I saved them. Then she had her Kindergarten feast on the Wednesday before Thanksgiving. As the head room mom, I was lucky enough to get to help out at the feast. They had an incredible spread! Turkey, stuffing, gravy, mashed potatoes, cranberry sauce, corn, jello, cornbread, rolls, pumpkin pie, apple pie and juice. The kids were all wearing their paper bag vests and homemade Indian headbands. Each vest and headband had pictures on them that told a story. Mrs. Cox gave them all "war paint" and then we served the meal. Their tables were all lined up to make one long table like the pilgrims and all the kids were really good about trying something new. Tori learned that she actually liked cranberry sauce, but her favorite dish was the pumpkin pie.

Baking Memories

by Madeline Arendt

As long as I can remember, baking homemade cookies and other goodies for the holidays has been a tradition in our family. There are always "favorite" baked goods that everyone looks forward to year after year. So, each year I begin my baking with the favorites, then add one or two new recipes to my baking repertoire. After taste-testing by the family, a few of the new recipes might even make it to "favorite" status. The family tradition continues as our grandchildren enjoy the process of "baking memories."

...from the Memorabilia Box...

Recipe cards

To the Layout...

For Both Pages:

1. Begin with 12″ × 12″ brown cardstock as the background for the pages.

2. Cut strips of red and green decorative papers about 3″, 2″, and 1″ wide. Place straight edges toward the outside of the page; form deckled edges on the other side by laying the deckle ruler over the paper and pulling up excess paper. Layer the decorative papers in red and green color ranges; where the strips meet at the corners, alternate each strip while gluing them down.

3. Cut two 14″ lengths of each ribbon. Place buttons at even spacing on ribbon—trees on red ribbons and hearts on green ribbons. Sew the buttons in place with needle and thread; if you do not sew, tie a thread through the button holes, then glue into place on the ribbon. Glue the ribbons over the layered paper strips. Fold the ends to the back side of the page and glue them.

4. Use a Sizzix machine to cut 2 large gingerbread men from kraft cardstock and 2 from brown foam. Glue the cardstock cutout onto the foam cutout, allowing a slight edge of the foam to show from beneath.

5. Use the cosmetic sponge and Vintage Photo ink to shade the edges of the cardstock cutout, giving the appearance of browned edges.

6. Run a bead of glitter paint around the edges of the cutout, including the hearts. Allow to dry.

7. Use the white paint to draw wavy icing lines onto the arms and legs of the cutout. Allow to dry.

8. Form a small bow from a piece of red baby rickrack. Glue onto cutout at neckline.

9. Repeat the process for the second gingerbread man cutout. Glue these large gingerbread men onto the layout at the corners.

10. Use a cotton swab with Fired Brick ink to apply a slight touch of color to the gingerbread men's cheeks.

11. Mat all the photos on white cardstock, about ⅛″ larger than the photos all around.

12. Make small gingerbread men for each corner of all the photos (4 times the number of photos). Punch out the gingerbread shapes from kraft cardstock. Sponge the Vintage Photo ink onto each to darken slightly. Use a small brush to paint the glitter onto each gingerbread man. Allow to dry, then brush a coat of the glass finish onto each to glaze. Allow to dry. Glue 1 small gingerbread man on each corner of the photos, angled to the center of each photo.

13. Glue the photos on the pages at various angles.

From Your Scrap Stash...

Cardstock, 12″ × 12″: Walnut Felt, Camel Hair Classic Laid, White Specs, kraft (DMD Ind.)

Decorative papers: Dear Santa Earthtones, Christmas Trees and Red Stars (American Traditional Designs); Blue Jean Teddy Paper, Green Gingham and Red Gingham (Paper Adventures); Red Stitched (Karen Foster Design); Sponge Sage (Frances Meyer); vellum, white

Crafter's Images Photo Fabric, cotton twill (Blumenthal Lansing)

Premium Photo Paper, gloss (Hewlett-Packard)

Ribbons: sheer/iridescent, ¼″, red; woven iridescent, ¼″, green (May Arts)

Embellishments: Christmas Past buttons (Doodlebug); label holder, large antique gold, rectangle (Making Memories); baby rickrack

Sticker collection, Christmas alphabet (American Traditional Designs)

Flexi-Foam, brown (Fibre-Craft)

Deckle Ruler (Plaid Ent./All Night Media)

FolkArt Papier Paints: White Pearl Metallic, Disco Glitter, Sepia Glass Finish (Plaid Ent./All Night Media)

Stamps: All Night Media alphabet set, Jive font (Plaid Ent.)

Stamping inks: Archival Ink, Jet Black; Tim Holtz Distress Ink, Antique Linen, Vintage Photo, Peeled Paint, and Fired Brick (Ranger Ind.)

Kraft paper corners, Classic (3L)

Screw brads (Karen Foster Design)

Crystal Stickers Bubble Alphabet, black (Mark Richards Enterprises, Inc.)

Adhesives: Zip Dry paper glue (Beacon Adhesives); Super Tape, ⅛″ and 1″ (Therm O Web)

18kt gold leafing pen (Krylon)

Tools: Sizzix die-cutting machine and dies, gingerbread man, square set, circles (Provo Craft); Paper Shaper punch, Ginger Man (EK Success); 12″ paper trimmer, Paper Edgers pinking and stamp cut scissors (Fiskars); brushes; sewing needle and thread; cosmetic sponge wedge; waxed cord

Left Page:

1. Cut shapes for the title letters using scraps of photo fabric and the smallest shape from the square and circle dies. Use a cosmetic sponge and Antique Linen ink to add some shading to the cutouts.

2. Brush the glitter paint onto each of the shapes. Allow to dry.

3. Press the letter stickers onto the shapes. Alternate the circles and squares for each letter in the title.

4. Use the white paint to outline the edges of each shape to represent icing. Allow to dry.

5. Glue the title letters onto the page near the top.

Right Page:

1. Make a file folder shape as a holder for the recipes; cut a 10″ × 6½″ rectangle from the white cardstock. Fold in half and trim off ½″ of the open edges, halfway across, to form the tab. Use the cosmetic sponge and Antique Linen ink to add slight "aging" to the edges of the folder.

2. Attach metal label holder to front of folder with screw brads. Touch the tops of the brads with the gold leafing pen to change the color. Add the alpha letter stickers to spell "RECIPES" inside the label holder.

3. From the Camel Hair cardstock, cut rectangles 6″ × 4½″ for each of your recipes. Scan or retype the recipes into your computer, keeping the area of type to no more than 5½″ wide and 4″ high. Print the recipes onto photo fabric, following the package directions. Cut the fabric recipes to fit the cards, leaving about a ⅛″ border all around. Adhere the recipes to the cards using the photo corners for appearance, but also use glue at each corner.

4. From photo fabric waste, cut a strip with pinking scissors. Stamp the strip with the black ink and alphabet the words "kid tested." Color the strip with all colors of the Distress Ink, using a sponge. The same coloring may be added to the edges of the recipes, if desired.

5. Computer generate other phrases and names for front of folder and print on vellum. Cut out with decorative scissors and glue into place on recipe holder.

6. Poke a hole on both side edges of holder, going completely through all layers of papers. Thread a piece of waxed cord through the holes. Tie a double knot on the top ends. Pull through to the back, leaving enough to have the holder open slightly. Then tie a knot at the back on each piece, and place a piece of tape over the ends on the back side to help hold in place.

7. Adhere 3 strips of 1″ Super Tape to the back of the recipe holder. Remove backing and place onto page.

8. A photo can be added to the front of the holder, if desired. Insert recipe cards in holder.

Kids' Stuff

Wouldn't it be wonderful to capture every special moment of childhood so you could remember it forever? Whether for your child or for yourself, memorabilia bring back those moments vividly. You can create scrapbook pages either with or without photos.

Handmade clothing shows the love of a parent or grandparent for a child—even those designer labels on favorite little clothes can recall fond memories. Spirit ribbons from the big game, sports and dance programs, and ticket stubs help tell the story of our school days.

Concerts and festivals enjoyed with friends serve as highlights of our lives. Kids' art is great to photograph or copy to use for everything from photo mats to page backgrounds. Even wrappers from the kids' favorite junk food add to the tale of their childhood, as told in your scrapbook.

Stitches of Love

by Jane Swanson

Glamorous store-bought doll clothes were all the rage when I was a child. My fashion doll had a complete wardrobe, but to my little girl dismay, all the clothes were all handmade garments my mother created for me. I played with them reluctantly, wishing for the "real thing." One of her creations, however, always caught my eye—I often chose the red polka-dot dress for my dark-haired doll. Today it is my joy to rediscover these hand-sewn treasures in my boxes of memorabilia. I now realize that these doll clothes are truly "stitches of love" from my mother.

...from the Memorabilia Box...

Handmade dress for fashion doll

To the Layout...

For Both Pages:

1. Straight stitch with a sewing machine and white thread around 3 sides each of two 12″ × 12″ pieces of red cardstock for the page backgrounds, about ¼″ in from the edges.

2. Zigzag stitch on four ⅜″ × 12″ red cardstock strips.

3. Cut two 2″ × 11½″ striped borders.

4. Cut two 8″ × 11½″ pieces of yellow cardstock.

5. Cut two 8″ × 11½″ pieces of vellum sewing pattern paper or actual pattern pieces.

6. Using the Print Clearly Dashed font, print title on polka-dot paper. Cut into 2″ × 11½″ strips.

7. Punch three ½″ red circles, three 1″ red circles, three 1″ polka-dot circles, and three 1½″ red circles.

8. Assemble the page backgrounds, starting with the stitched red backgrounds, placing them with the unstitched edges together. Attach polka-dot title strips to red backgrounds, slightly below stitching across top of page and meeting in the middle. Attach striped paper to bottom of red background, slightly above the stitching at the bottom of the page. Glue pattern paper over the yellow cardstock; center these between the borders at top and bottom of page, meeting in the middle and leaving a red stitched area on the outside of the page.

9. Attach zigzag strips horizontally over the seams between the dotted and striped borders and the yellow pattern-covered center area.

10. Attach punched circles, pins, snaps, and needle and thread with Glue Dots on borders.

Left Page:

1. Mat focal point photo of doll and wardrobe on white, then red.

2. Attach dress with red ribbon and white brads at center and Glue Dots at shoulders and ends of skirt.

3. Add ribbons to left of title block.

Right Page:

1. Mat the other 2 photos of doll and accessories on red and glue to background.

2. Type journaling and print on vellum. Glue over pattern paper.

From Your Scrap Stash...

Cardstock: Red Multi-Stack (Die Cuts With A View), Canary Yellow (Bazzill Basics)

Patterned papers: polka-dot and stripe (Over the Moon Press); vellum "sewing pattern" paper (Club Scrap)

Brads (The Happy Hammer)

Red woven ribbon (Offray)

Sewing supplies: glass-headed pins; snaps; needle; white thread; sewing machine

Font: Print Clearly Dashed (Blue Vinyl Fonts)

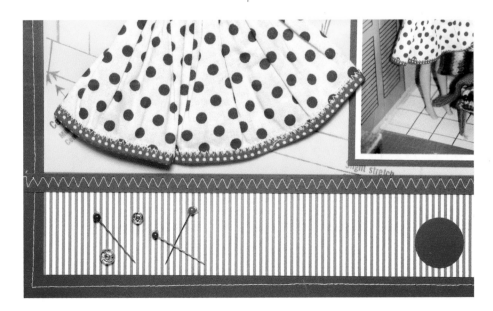

Football Champs

by Betsy H. Edwards

High school football is BIG in Texas, and it's even BIGGER when your school wins the state championship! In 1958, our team won it all. I still remember the excitement; the pep rallies; the games; the cool, crisp air; and the fun of being part of an amazing season. Fortunately, I saved lots of memorabilia. You can recreate these pages with your own high school sports keepsakes. Share the pleasures of your school days and relive the exhilaration each time you open your scrapbook.

...from the Memorabilia Box...

Sports programs, ticket stubs, spirit ribbons

To the Layout...

For Both Pages:

1. I was inspired by the torn edges of the ticket stubs to use no scissors in this project—I tore all mats and page elements, except those that were die-cut.

2. Place a 12″ × 12″ sheet of each of your school colors in front of you. Tear away one-third of each sheet. Tear a strip about ⅜″ wide and 12″ long from each torn section. Adhere each ⅓-page torn sheet on top of a whole sheet of the opposite color. Adhere the 12″ × ⅜″ strips to the opposite color paper—see photo.

3. Gather photos, letters, embellishments, and memorabilia. Experiment with placement of memorabilia on the double-page spread. Start with larger items such as programs. Then add spirit ribbons. Tear mats for photos from remaining cardstock, allowing about ¼″ to ½″ borders around photos, and trying unusual shapes such as the sunburst design. When you are happy with your placement, glue or tape in place. ,

Left Page:

1. Select an appropriate color and font for your journaling. Print on white paper. Tear a mat from one of the school colors. Place white paper on top of mat and punch 2 holes in the top, through both layers, above the writing. Run 12″ of grosgrain ribbon and 8″ of metallic ribbon through the 2 holes and tie in front. Adhere to page.

2. Add "Champs" title letters, football die-cut, and helmet charm.

3. Glue ticket stubs here and there on page.

From Your Scrap Stash...

Cardstock: 12″ × 12″, solid-color cardstock (3 sheets of each of your 2 school colors)

White computer paper

Adhesives: acid-free double-stick tape (Therm O Web); Xyron machine with permanent adhesive cartridge (Xyron)

Die-cuts: letters "C", "H", "A", "M", "P", and "S" in Sizzix Fun Serif lower-case font; year "1958" in Sizzix Playground font; football (Provo Craft)

Stickers: Essentials football and football shoes (Sandylion)

Charm: Li'l Charms, football helmet (American Traditional Designs)

Ribbon: ⅛″ metallic ribbon, 16″, in one school color; ⅜″ grosgrain ribbon, 12″, in second school color

Hole punch, ¼″ round

Tools: pencil; scissors

High school football is BIG in Texas. Winning the state championship is even bigger!! 1958 was a banner year for my school — we won it all. We were the state AAAA champs. I remember bus caravans and even reserved cars on a train for out of town playoff games. Pep rallies, spirit ribbons, game programs, chrysanthemum corsages tied with blue & gold ribbons, cheering, sucking on a lemon to soothe a throat sore from yelling ...

MEMORIES

Right Page:

1. Embellish page with die-cut date and stickers.

2. Glue ticket stubs here and there on page.

3. Use remaining metallic ribbon to accent pages.

A Day at Shea

Out to the Ball Game

by Kathi Rerek

What's better than a wonderful day at the ballpark with your kids? My daughter, Rebecca, a die-hard Mets fan, had been given tickets to see a game at Shea Stadium, and after much anticipation we were on our way to the ball game. Of course, I took lots of photos to document the great ballpark, our seats up close to the players, and the continual thrill and excitement on my daughter's face. I knew I'd want to commemorate this day in our scrapbook, so I kept copies of the tickets and the stubs to use in this layout.

...from the Memorabilia Box...

Ticket copies and ticket stubs

From Your Scrap Stash...

Papers: Dawson Alaska Blue, 2 sheets; Amber Glow, Polka-Dot, and Variegated Stripe (BasicGrey)

Tim Holtz Distress Inks, Black Soot (Ranger Ind,)

Die-cutting hand tool and Marisa font dies (QuickKutz)

Dymo embossing labeler and label roll, blue, ⅜" wide (Dymo div. of Esselte Corp.)

HammerMill 4 mil inkjet transparencies (International Paper)

Xyron machine with adhesive cartridge (Xyron)

To the Layout...

For Both Pages:

1. Use the blue papers as the backgrounds for the pages.

2. Cut two 3" x 12" strips from the striped paper. Ink the edges with the black ink.

3. Adhere the borders vertically along the outside edges of each of the pages.

4. Crop all the photos and mat on Amber paper, about ⅛" larger all around than the photos.

5. Ink the edges of all photo mats with the black ink, and glue them to the backgrounds.

6. Cut the title letters from the Amber paper using the QuickKutz tool. Ink the edges of the die-cut letters. Glue in place on the background.

Left Page:

1. Mat the focal photo first on Amber, then on Polka-Dot, and finally on Amber again. Ink the edges of all 3 mats with black. Adhere the triple-matted focal photo to the top left of the page.

2. Adhere the tickets directly onto the photo at the bottom corner of the page.

3. Cut a transparency to the size of the photo and place over the photo and tickets.

4. Use the labeler to create the journaling for the memorabilia pocket. Attach at bottom of photo, adhering transparency to background at same time.

5. Add plain labeler tape to the side edges of the transparency, adhering it to the page and forming a pocket.

Right Page:

1. Use the labeler to create the journaling at upper right.

2. Adhere the tape journaling to a piece of Amber paper. Edge the Amber paper with black ink.

3. Mat the journaling block with the Polka-Dot paper. Ink the edges of the Polka-Dot paper.

4. Mat again with Amber, and ink those edges. Glue to upper right of page by title.

5. Adhere additional journaling to a vertical strip of Amber paper; cut pieces of Polka-Dot paper and glue near top and bottom across strip. Edge with black ink, and glue between photos.

Rock Concert

by Lea Cioci

What a thrill! This summer concert "On the Waterfront" in Rockford, Illinois, was a big hit. All the teens were having fun watching the band Vertical Horizon, dancing to the music, and enjoying the sweet freedom of summer vacation. To serve as reminders of this exciting day, I've incorporated clippings on the band, lyrics to a favorite song, memorabilia clipped from the program and ads, the well-worn concert area map, and, of course, photos of friends in attendance.

...from the Memorabilia Box...

Clippings, concert ads and program, map of venue

To the Layout...

For Both Pages:

1. The color-block papers make the layout simple for scrapping. Each page has a darker background and squares, rectangles, or circles of a lighter hue of the same color placed on the page to create a layout pattern; it looks like vellum has been layered onto the background. While you can scrap your items on each shape, you can also cover a shape if you want or even use two shapes as one, as I've done in the upper left corner for the map.

2. Decide where you want all your pictures and memorabilia to go, arranging them on the pages in a pleasing manner but not gluing down yet.

Left Page:

1. Once the basic placement has been decided, print a computer-generated title on coordinating paper and glue in place.

2. The photo on the lower left was given a contrasting color mat that is quite a bit larger than the photo.

3. Adhere photos and memorabilia to the page using adhesive dots and/or the tape runner. Adhere the map using Zots, so the map is slightly lifted from the page for additional dimension.

4. Glue the ticket to a purple tag. Using an awl or paper piercer, make a hole in the page and attach the tag with a brad.

5. Punch holes on each side of the quote on the bottom right, and insert a brad on each side for a nice decorative touch.

6. The image stickers and word sticker are added to further embellish the page. The kiss sticker looks like it was really kissed on the band's photo!

7. For a final trim, and to carry out the contrasting color scheme of the 2-page spread, run a line of purple Sticky Stitches along the bottom of this page.

From Your Scrap Stash...

Color-blocked papers in green and purple, 6″ × 6″ squares (All My Memories)

Adhesives: Sticky Dots and Craft Zots (Therm O Web) or Xyron Cheetah tape runner (Xyron)

Sizzix machine and alphabet dies (Provo Craft)

Sticky Stitches, purple and green (Colorbök)

Die-cut guitar (Li'l Davis Designs)

Quotes (Making Memories)

Stickers

Tools: awl or paper piercer; large circle punch or circle cutter (Fiskars)

Hangin' Out

Right Page:

1. Use color-block paper in a contrasting color for this page. This color block not only has squares and rectangles but a circle as well, for an interesting element. Print computer-generated lyrics to one of the band's songs on white paper with a small title strip; personal journaling is printed on coordinating paper and glued at the lower right. Each printed piece is cut to fit the color-block space and glued in place.

2. For the round photo, use a large circle punch or a circle cutting tool. Also cut a circle mat of green paper to contrast with the purple page and make the image pop out.

3. Adhere all the photos and memorabilia from the festival program using adhesive dots and/or the tape runner. Cut a small picture to glue inside the matchbook embellishment at the upper right; the photo is an element of surprise, which can only be seen when the matchbook cover is flipped open.

4. Die-cut the word "ROCK" and place along the upper right edge of the page.

5. Once all the photos and memorabilia are adhered to the page, use stickers to further embellish the page. The guitar die-cut sticker adds dimension.

6. For a final trim, and to carry out the color scheme, run a line of green Sticky Stitches along the bottom of the page.

Pool Party

by Jan Monahan

My family gets together every time something happens. Weddings, funerals, and births are a given, but we get together for not-so-important happenings as well. This particular gathering was to celebrate a new home my brother and his wife had just purchased. The babies were enjoying Moon Pies, getting more on the outside than in, so we cooled and cleaned them in the wading pool. We applied a liberal coating of sunscreen to their tender baby skin, since they decided "birthday suits" were better than bathing suits.

...from the Memorabilia Box...

Moon Pie wrappers, Coppertone label

From Your Scrap Stash...

To the Layout...

For Both Pages:

1. Use light blue cardstock for backgrounds. Randomly stamp over both pages with stamps of feet and hands in blue ink.

2. Trim photos to crop for best composition.

3. Die-cut letters from red cardstock with machine.

4. Arrange the letters on yellow cardstock and cut the yellow title banner to size.

5. Put all items in need of adhesive through Xyron machine: pie wrappers, sunscreen label, pictures, letters, and yellow banner; press into place on the layout. Keep the layout loose and fun.

Left Page:

Cut a yellow crescent moon and white full moons, and journal by hand to tell the story of the celebration. Run through Xyron and press into place, overlapping photos and memorabilia.

Right Page:

The scrapbooking buttons come on a card with adhesive preapplied. Remove paper backing and press buttons into place at lower right.

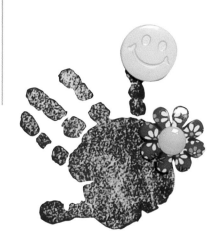

POOL PARTY

About the Editor

JAN MOLLET EVANS

Jan Mollet Evans holds a master of arts in teaching and began her career teaching art and English in public schools. Since the 1980s, she has worked in the creative industry as an advertising and public relations director, freelance writer, and project designer for many books and magazines, and as an independent marketing consultant. Jan's work has given her the opportunity to collaborate with many of the best designers in the creative industry, and she is proud to present some of their work to you in this book.

About the Designers

The talented designers contributing layouts for this book represent a wide range of ages, family situations, geographies, vocations, and creative backgrounds. Their love of scrapbooking speaks volumes, but here is a bit more about each one of them.

PAM ARCHER

As a child, Pam would play for hours with fabric scraps. She fell in love with sewing, so it's no surprise that she earned a degree in clothing/textiles. She pursued a career in retail, then served as a pattern company spokesperson. Now Pam is a freelance writer with a book on fabric bags and many magazine articles to her credit.

MADELINE ARENDT

Madeline has worked as a freelance designer in the creative craft industry for over five years, with many projects published in magazines. She not only designs for creative companies, but loves to teach others how to make the projects she conceives. Madeline enjoys family life with her retired husband, children, and grandchildren.

KRISTEN S. BABEL

Kristen is an avid crafter who concentrates mainly on scrapbooking and paper crafts. A single mom, she adopted her son Alekandro at two days old. Her scrapbooking and journaling documents his life to help him understand his journey into her life, where he came from, who he is, and how many people love him.

ANNETTE BAILEY

Annette is a nationally known writer and designer specializing in scrapbooking, paper crafts, sewing, and embroidery. Through her company, Simple Solutions, she performs writing, editing, project management, and multimedia tasks. With a husband and two children, Annette loves having her office in her Midwestern home.

LEA CIOCI

Projects by Lea can be found in magazine articles, ads, and how-to books. In addition to her work as a freelance designer, she serves as demo artist, instructor, consultant, and product developer for several companies in the creative industry. For fifteen years, she has taught at an area college, stamp stores, conventions, and retreats.

KATHE CUNNINGHAM

"Scrapbooking fulfills my need to be creative, fuels my love of photography, and stimulates my inner writer," explains Kathe. Her work has been featured in many publications and promotional pieces for manufacturers. When she's not busy with her husband and three sons, Kathe teaches at a scrapbook store and serves on several design teams.

BECKY DEZARN

Becky lives in rural Indiana, and her favorite scrapbook subjects are her husband and two boys. In addition to scrapbooking, she also enjoys other creative paper crafts such as card making and altered art. Becky began scrapbooking in the spring of 2000 and since then has contributed to several design teams and publications.

BETSY H. EDWARDS

Betsy served as president of the Society of Decorative Painters and has work in the permanent collections of the Smithsonian, the White House, the Library of Congress, and more. With diverse abilities, Betsy is an education coordinator, certified craft designer and demonstrator, author, consultant, TV talent, and tireless volunteer.

SUE ELDRED

For several years, Sue owned her own rubber stamp and scrapbook store and enjoyed teaching classes there. Since closing her store, she has happily worked as a designer for several manufacturers in the creative industry. Sue lives in Illinois with her husband and three children and loves to create projects in her home studio/office.

MICHELE EMERSON-ROBERTS

Michele is a multifaceted designer with a love of paper/book arts, beading, polymer clay, and painting. Although she's an award-winning painter, her favorite design medium has always been paper—molded, cut, pierced, painted, folded, glued, or torn. Michele shares her Arizona home with her husband, a dog, and three cats.

KITTY FOSTER

A stay-at-home mom with four children, Kitty says, "My obsession with scrapbooking began nine years ago at an in-home demonstration. I was attracted to the idea of preserving my precious photos, but later realized that the creative outlet keeps me coming back for more." Her projects are seen in many publications and websites.

MADELINE FOX

Quilting, cross-stitching, drawing, and painting are some of the many arts and crafts Madeline enjoys. But when she discovered scrapbooking, it appealed to both her artistic side and her sentimental "preserve-the-past, celebrate-the-present" side as well. She collects ephemera for her pages and loves papers with a vintage feel.

LINDA TURNER GRIEPENTROG

Working from her home outside Portland, Oregon, Linda runs her own company, G Wiz Creative Services. She does writing, editing, designing, teaching, and touring for sewing industry companies. With her dogs as constant companions, she loves creating in her sewing room. Amazingly, this is her first scrapbooking project!

CARLA JACOBSON

Carla was born and raised in Southern California, but her family relocated to Missouri, where, she attended high school and college. Carla moved once again, to Nashville in 1994, and gave birth to a son, Cooper. Scrapbooking since 1997, she designs for several companies and has been published in a variety of books and magazines.

SUSAN I. JONES

Specializing in one-of-a-kind fiber and paper art for more than 25 years, Susan has designed and produced costumes and sets for the theater and dance, as well as art for advertising and set design. Published in seven books and many fiber-related art magazines, her mixed media art is often featured to promote new products.

SARA KENDRICK

Sara began scrapping eight years ago after her first baby arrived. Now a stay-at-home mom, she resides with her husband and three children in Texas. Sara feels that her "love of photography and writing are a perfect fit with scrapbooking; it's become part of daily life." She teaches scrapping, and her work appears in books and on the Net.

CATHERINE MACE

At their store, Cathy and her husband teach classes on all aspects of papercrafting: making books and boxes, origami, tea bag folding, handmade cards, paper tole, scrapbooking, and rubber stamping. Their company, *Papers by Catherine,* specializes in imported papers. Cathy is author of many books and articles on papercrafting.

SHARON MANN

Sharon's passion is designing with needle and thread, but she also experiments with a variety of other creative products. She blends traditional needlecrafts with a range of craft techniques to produce novel, dimensional artwork. Currently her artistic endeavors include fiber arts, beading, doll making, and altered art.

WENDY MCKEEHAN

Like many people, Wendy began scrapbooking shortly after her son was born. She feels that it "took a long time to learn to be creative," but now she loves to create pages for her family. Wendy shares her passion by teaching classes, doing demos at trade shows, and contributing to many different idea books and magazines.

JAN MONAHAN

Jan has been crafting since she can remember. Her design career began in 2001 with a project published in a magazine. "My scrapbooking started as just pictures on a page and blossomed from there," she explains. Now, Jan has over 36 designs in magazines and books and enjoys getting paid for doing what she loves to do.

STACEY MORGAN

"I feel very blessed to be able to work in the creative field," says Stacey. "I have worked craft shows for many years, taught classes, demonstrated products, developed innovative products, and written instructions for creative magazines. I have also had the pleasure of writing two books on my specialty, polymer clay."

KATHI REREK

Kathi's layouts most frequently feature her daughter, Rebecca, and her two cats. She also likes to use her collection of scrapping supplies and tools to make cards and tags. Currently, she is a member of two design teams and has had several layouts published. When not scrapping, Kathi enjoys photography, reading, and traveling.

PATTI SWOBODA

Author, designer, and inventor of scrapbook products and techniques, Patti has appeared on PBS scrapbooking programs and enjoys "makin' scrappin' happen!" She loves scrapping with family and says, "It's a great way for us to connect. I've learned so much about them, and we have such a good time together."

ELAINA PECORA

For over 35 years, Elaina has been designing and teaching. As a public school teacher and principal, she encouraged her students and faculty to pursue the arts, because "creative activities stimulate learning." Elaina specializes in paper arts, collage, and florals, but says her "greatest creations" are her sons and grandchildren.

HEIDI SMITH

A Navy wife, Heidi has enjoyed creative endeavors all her life. "I've been scrapbooking since my husband and I were married," she shares. "I also enjoy cooking, shopping, reading, and spending time with hubby when he is not at sea. I'm trying to better my photography skills, with my husband and dog as my unwilling subjects."

MICHAELA YOUNG-MITCHELL

Michaela has been scrapbooking for six years, and her layouts have appeared in almost every scrapping magazine. Her work has been recognized in many layout contests, and she serves as a design team member and contributor for several companies. Michaela's favorite scrapping subjects are her daughter and son.

JANE SWANSON

Jane and her pastor husband have been married for 28 years and have six children and a grandson. She majored in interior design/art in college, but when she discovered scrapbooking, she says, "all my artistic passions came together. Best of all, this hobby has introduced me to fabulous scrapping women all over the world."

Resource List

The following companies manufactured supplies used in the layouts in this book, but are in no way associated with or endorsed by C&T Publishing. Every effort has been made to make the list complete for easy product sourcing. Check your local scrapbook shop or craft retailer for these products.

1001 Fonts
www.1001fonts.com

3L Corporation
847-808-6071
www.scrapbook-adhesives.com

3M Stationery Products Division
800-328-6276
www.3m.com

7gypsies
877-749-7797
www.sevengypsies.com

Adhesive Technologies, Inc.
603-926-1616
www.adhesivetech.com

All My Memories
801-619-8808
www.allmymemories.com

Altered Pages
405-360-1185
www.alteredpages.com

American Tag Co.
800-223-3956
www.americantag.net

American Traditional Designs
603-942-8100
www.americantraditional.com

ANW Crestwood
800-525-3196 www.anwcrestwood.com

Art Institute Glitter, Inc.
928-639-0805
www.artglitter.com

ARTchix Studio
250-370-9985
www.artchixstudio.com

Artistic Wire
630-530-7567
www.artisticwire.com

BasicGrey
801-451-6006
www.basicgrey.com

Bazzill Basics Paper
480-558-8557
www.bazzillbasics.com

Beacon Adhesives Co.
914-699-3400
www.beaconcreates.com

The Beadery Craft Products
401-539-2432
www.thebeadery.com

Blue Moon Beads/Elizabeth Ward Co.
800-377-6715
www.bluemoonbeads.com

Blue Vinyl Fonts
www.bvfonts.com

Blumenthal Lansing Co.
201-935-6220
www.blumenthallansing.com

Canson, Inc.
413-538-9250
www.canson-us.com

Charming Thoughts
877-467-8995
www.charmingthoughts.com

Chatterbox, Inc.
888-416-6260
www.chatterboxinc.com

Chuck E. Cheese's
(CEC Entertainment, Inc.)
972-258-8507
www.chuckecheese.com

Clearsnap
360-293-6634
www.clearsnap.com

Club Scrap
888-634-9100
www.clubscrap.com

Colorbök, Inc.
800-366-4660
www.colorbok.com

Crafter's Pick Adhesive Products
510-526-7616
www.crafterspick.com

Craf-T Products, Inc.
507-235-3996
www.craf-tproducts.com

Creating Keepsakes
801-495-7200
www.creatingkeepsakes.com

Creative Imaginations, Inc.
800-942-6487
www.cigift.com

Creative Memories
www.creativememories.com

Crescent Cardboard Company, LLC
800-323-1055
www.crescentcardboard.com

The Daisy Bucket
541-571-8685
www.daisybucket.com

Darice, Inc.
440-238-9150,
www.darice.com

DecoArt
606-365-3193
www.decoart.com

Delta Technical Coatings, Inc.
562-695-7969
www.deltacrafts.com

Design Originals
817-877-0067
www.d-originals.com

Die Cuts With A View
801-224-6766
www.dcwv.com

DMC Corp.
973-589-0606
www.dmc-usa.com

DMD Industries, Inc.
800-727-2727
www.dmdind.com

Doodlebug Design, Inc.
801-952-0555
www.doodlebug.ws

Duncan Enterprises
559-291-4444
www.duncancrafts.com

Dymo (div. of Esselte Corporation)
www.dymo.com

EK Success
800-524-1349
www.eksuccess.com

Ellison/Sizzix
949-598-8822
www.ellison.com

Epson America, Inc.
800-GoEpson
www.epson.com

FiberMark
802-258-2747
www.scrapbooking.fibermark.com

Fibers by the Yard
405-364-8066
www.fibersbytheyard.com

Fiber Scraps
215-230-4905
www.fiberscraps.com

Fibre-Craft Materials Corp.
847-647-1140
www.fibrecraft.com

Fiskars Brands, Inc.
715-842-2091
www.fiskars.com

Frances Meyer (div. of Chartpak)
413-584-5446
www.francesmeyer.com

Galloping Horse Productions
503-846-0708
www.gallopinghorseproductions.com

Glue Dots International
888-688-7131
www.gluedots.com

The Happy Hammer
720-870-5248
www.thehappyhammer.com

Heidi Grace Designs
253-735-9008
www.heidigrace.com

Henkel Consumer Adhesives, Inc.
440-937-7350
www.duckproducts.com

Hero Arts Rubber Stamps, Inc.
510-652-6055
www.heroarts.com

Hewlett-Packard
www.hpshopping.com

Hunt Manufacturing
215-656-0300
www.hunt-corp.com

HyGloss Products
800-444-9456
www.hygloss.com

Impress Rubber Stamps
206-526-5818
www.impressrubberstamps.com

Inkadinkado
800-523-8452
www.inkadinkado.com

International Paper Co.
www.hammermill.com

Jest Charming
702-564-5101
www.jestcharming.com

JHB International, Inc.
303-751-8100
www.buttons.com

Jo-Ann Stores
www.joann.com

JudiKins, Inc.
310-515-1115
www.judikins.com

K & Company
816-389-4150
www.kandcompany.com

Karen Foster Design
801-451-9779
www.karenfosterdesign.com

KI Memories
972-243-5595
www.kimemories.com

Krause Publications (KP Books)
715-445-2214
www.krause.com

Krylon
800-797-3332
www.krylon.com

Lettering Delights
(div. of Inspire Graphics)
www.letteringdelights.com

Li'l Davis Designs
949-838-0344
www.lildavisdesigns.com

Magic Scraps
972-238-1838
www.magicscraps.com

Making Memories
801-294-0430
www.makingmemories.com

Mark Richards Enterprises, Inc.
631-342-0091
www.markrichardsusa.com

Ma Vinci's Reliquary
www.crafts.dm.net/mall/reliquary

May Arts
203-637-8366
www.mayarts.com

McGill, Inc.
815-568-7244
www.mcgillinc.com

Michaels Stores, Inc.
www.michaels.com

Mrs. Grossman's Paper Co.
707-763-1700
www.mrsgrossmans.com

Offray Ribbon Co.
570-752-5934
www.offray.com

Once Upon a Scribble
435-628-8577
www.onceuponascribble.com

Over the Moon Press
(available through EK Success)

Paper Adventures
(div. of The Paper Co.)
800-727-0699
www.paperadventures.com

The Paper Company/ANW Crestwood
800-525-3196
www.anwcrestwood.com

Paper Inspirations
406-756-9677
www.paperinspirations.com

Paper Mojo
800-420-3818
www.papermojo.com

Papers by Catherine
713-723-3334
www.papersbycatherine.com

Paper Studio
www.paperstudio.com.au

Pebbles, Inc.
801-235-1520
www.pebblesinc.com

PFY Rubber Stamps
www.pfy.com

Pioneer Photo Albums, Inc.
818-882-2161
www.pioneerphotoalbums.com

Plaid Enterprises, Inc./All Night Media
678-291-8100
www.plaidonline.com

Printed Treasures by Milliken
www.milliken.com

Provo Craft/Sizzix
801-794-9000
www.provocraft.com

Prym Dritz
864-576-5050
www.dritz.com

PSX Design (div. of Duncan Ent.)
559-291-4444
www.psxdesign.com

Pure Allure
760-966-3650

Purple Onion Designs
www.purpleoniondesigns.com

QuicKutz, Inc.
801-765-1144
www.quickutz.com

Ranger Industries
732-389-3535
www.rangerink.com

RS Industrial
770-844-1748
www.fixallstickkit.com

Rusty Pickle
801-746-1045
www.rustypickle.com

Sandylion Sticker Designs
905-475-0523
www.sandylion.com

Sanford Corp.
800-323-0749
www.prismacolor.com

Scenic Route Paper Company
801-785-0761
www.scenicroutepaper.com

Scrapworks
801-363-1010
www.scrapworks.com

SEI
435-752-4142
www.shopsei.com

Simplicity
888-588-2700
www.simplicity.com

Stampendous
714-688-0288
www.stampendous.com

Stampin' Up!
800-782-6787
www.stampinup.com

Stewart Superior Corp.
800-558-2875
www.stewartsuperior.com

Superior Threads
800-499-1777
www.superiorthreads.com

Tara Materials, Inc.
770-963-5256
www.taramaterials.com

Therm O Web, Inc.
800-323-0799
www.thermoweb.com

Tombow
678-318-3344
www.tombowusa.com

Tsukineko
425-883-7733
www.tsukineko.com

Two Peas in a Bucket
608-827-0852
www.twopeasinabucket.com

Uchida of America
310-793-2200
www.uchida.com

Uptown Design Company
253-925-1234
www.uptowndesign.com

USArtQuest
517-522-6225
www.usartquest.com

Westrim Crafts
800-727-2727
www.westrimcrafts.com

Worldwood Industries
www.world-wood.com

Xyron (div. of Esselte Corp.)
480-443-9419
www.xyron.com

Great Titles from C&T PUBLISHING